What is *Riddle Rooms*?

Riddle Rooms is a dungeon designer's sourcebook which can be used to enhance any adventure. Each room contains a riddle, puzzle or challenge which your players must overcome in order to solve the room. Because the obstacles presented in these rooms require thinking and problem solving, characters of any ability or skill level will be equally challenged.

Dungeon Dilemmas is the first in the *Riddle Rooms* series. The rooms here are designed for use in dungeon settings.

Components

- *Dungeon Designer's Handbook*: This has all the information which you, as the dungeon designer, need to know. Each *Dungeon Dilemma* is described along with its solution and ideas for monsters and treasure.

- 22 *Player Information Sheets*: These playing aids are given to the players when they reach a place in your Dungeon where you've put a Dilemma. Some Dilemmas require more than one sheet -- this is noted in the *Dungeon Designer* information for that Dilemma. These sheets let the players know what can be seen in the room.

- 5 *Bonus Riddles*: These are individual riddles not contained within a room. They are found at the back of the Dungeon Designer's Handbook and on tear out sheets. These riddles are for you to use however you please.

- 1 *Riddle Item:* Riddle Items are magic items that have a riddle associated with them. Solving the riddle will give the players clues about what the item can do and how to use the item. Riddle Items may take many components to be useful and so give players a long term riddle to solve as part of a campaign.

How To Use Riddle Rooms In Your Game

Riddle Rooms will fit into any adventure, any gaming system. Place a *Riddle Room* anywhere in your dungeon! When your players encounter the *Riddle Room* give them the Player information sheet for that room. As the party tries to solve the room, refer to the *Handbook* for all the details.

The *Dungeon Designer Handbook* explains how each room should be solved. Every room contains enough information to be solved by even the weakest party. No special abilities or spells are required, and you may choose to have magic not work in some rooms to encourage your players to triumph with their wits, not by brute force. Several of the rooms require the players to have a few common items, such as water, oil, and so on. Check the Players Need section for the room to make sure your players have a way of solving the room. If a room doesn't have a Players Need section, then everything they need is in the room already.

How To Use The Dungeon Designer's Handbook

In the top corner of the explanation of a Dilemma are one or more symbols. These symbols are an easy way to see what your players get from the room. Use this to decide where you want to put a Dilemma.

Doorway: the solution to the puzzle will give the players access to a new part of your dungeon.

Treasure: when the players solve the dilemma they will get some treasure. You may reward them with whatever treasure is appropriate to your campaign. The *Handbook* lists some suggestions for treasures that relate to the theme of the Dilemma.

Special Treasure: these treasures are part of the Dilemma. Feel free to adjust their value or capabilities to match your campaign.

Person: when the players solve the room, they will meet a person. You can give these people whatever special capabilities or statistics you feel are appropriate.

The first part of each Dilemma is a description of what the players see. You may choose to read this to the party or let them work solely from the *Player Information Sheet*.

The next section is **Dungeon Designer Information**. This tells you how the Dilemma can be solved, and what happens if the players fall for any of the room's traps!

The <u>Monster</u> section explains any monsters the players may have to fight in the room. Monsters do one or two types of damage:

Minor A player should be able to take minor damage up to ten times without dying.

Moderate Players should be able to take moderate damage no more than three or four times.

If our description of a monster disagrees with your idea of how that monster should act, feel free to change its statistics.

The <u>Special Treasure</u> section details the abilities and uses of any Special Treasure in the room.

The <u>Treasure</u> section gives some ideas for interesting treasures that are appropriate to the room.

The <u>Players Need</u> tells you what items or abilities a party will need. Be sure your party can get these before entering the dungeon, or else make the items available somewhere in it.

Remember - these rooms are here for <u>you</u> to put in <u>your</u> dungeon! Feel free to change the contents, monsters and treasures as you like to fit into <u>your</u> adventure and role-playing system. Have fun!

Riddle Rooms™ #1 - Dungeon Dilemmas co-developed by RiddleMaster Games and Cloud Kingdom Games, Inc.
RiddleMaster Design team - Rick Smith, Darryl See, Robin Marks, Jason Glor.
Cloud Kingdom Design Team - Matt, Michelle, Rod, Vicky and Graptor.
Cover art by Dan Frazier. Interior artwork by Rod Stephens.

TABLE OF CONTENTS

Den of the Devourer

Dilemma #1

This room contains a bed, desk, chair, and small fireplace. Over the fireplace hangs a rusty sword and an axe. On the desk is an open diary. All the pages are stuck together and crack as you touch the diary, but the top page is legible. It says:

Provider, devourer,
A double-edged blade,
Man he has tamed her,
Accepting this trade.
Ravenously hungry,
Must all the time feed,
Yet drink she must not,
This can kill her indeed.

Dungeon Designer Information

The answer to the riddle is *fire*. To solve this room the players should light a fire in the fireplace. When the smoke from the fire starts up the chimney, two bats hidden there will fly away. As the fire burns, a glowing arrow will appear in the back of the fireplace pointing to a small break in the mortar. When this spot is pressed a small compartment up near where the bats were will pop open revealing the treasure.

Monsters

Bats — There are two large bats living in the chimney. If a player sticks an arm, torch or anything else into the chimney, the bats will come out into the room and attack. The bats will bite causing minor damage. They are very fast and hard to hit.

Treasure

Magic flint

When struck with steel, the flint produces a spark which will light any small combustible material, no matter how wet.

Magic soot

When tossed in the air, this forms a cloud of darkness in a 3' x 3' area. No one can see in or out of this cloud.

Magic stick

This is a small piece of wood which ignites easily, burns brightly, gives off heat, but is never consumed.

Players Need

Ability to start a fire

Dilemma #2

The Impervious Cube

In the center of this 35' x 20' room is a massive cube of dark gray stone with a statue of a Griffin perched on top. Leading up to the pedestal is a torn and faded 10' x 20' rug.

Inlaid on the front of the cube in silver letters is:

Relaxed I sit upon my perch
Till suddenly I give a lurch
And off I speed on wing-tips three
Before my prey can think to flee.
I make its flesh and tendons part
And claw my way into its heart.

Now only kin can set me free
So strike this cube with one of me.

Dungeon Designer Information

The answer to the riddle is *arrow.* To solve this room the players must strike the cube with an arrow. When they do this, the mouth of the Griffin will open wide, revealing the treasure concealed within the body of the statue. The mouth of the Griffin can not be opened by any other means. Players tapping on the body of the Griffin may detect that it is hollow.

<u>Special Treasure</u>

Five Arrows of Far Slaying

These have double the range and do triple the damage of normal arrows.

Five Arrows of Piercing

Nothing can block these arrows from their intended target. They will pierce anything (stone, trees, armor) between them and their quarry. The arrows have normal range and do normal damage.

Five Heat Seeking Arrows

If these miss their intended target, they will continue to fly up to five times normal range and attack the nearest source of heat. These arrows do normal damage.

<u>Players Need</u>

An arrow

In front of you is a large, heavy stone door. Strange buzzing and chirping sounds can be heard through the stone. The following words are carved into the door:

Rust Demise and Fire's Mirth,
Water Walker, Squeaking Dearth,
Wear me now upon your skin
And safely you may enter in.

Upon opening the door you see a 30' x 20' room. The floors, walls and ceiling of the room seem to writhe. Closer examination reveals that they are covered with insects crawling, hopping, jumping and flying from every visible surface. No details of the floor can be discerned under the knee deep layer of bugs.

Dungeon Designer Information

The answer to the riddle is *oil*. To solve this room, the players must coat themselves with oil before entering the room. The bugs will avoid any player wearing oil on his skin or garments, and will also run away from oil if it is spilled or thrown into the room.

Any player entering the room who is *not* coated in oil will be swarmed by bugs. The bugs do minor damage and make it impossible for the players to find anything in the room.

There is a large hole in floor of the room directly opposite the door along the rear wall. This contains the treasure. The hole is completely covered by bugs, but if a player covered with oil walks near, the bugs will scamper away and the treasure will be obvious.

Monsters

Bugs These bugs are annoying, jumping into the eyes ears and mouths of anyone not coated with oil, causing minor damage. It is *impossible* for players not wearing oil to find any treasure. The players will not be able to empty the room of bugs by any means.

Treasure

Scroll of Insect Summoning

This defensive spell summons a hoard of insects from this room which swarm between the caster and an enemy making the foe unable to attack the spell-caster.

Wand of Webs

This wand shoots out a web which will entangle a human sized opponent.

Beetle shell armor

This high quality armor is light, tough and completely resistant to acid.

Players Need

Oil

Dilemma #4

The Greenhouse Effect

This 15' x 20' chamber has a simple dirt floor. The ceiling is crumbly and bits of rock and gravel are strewn on the floor. Along the right hand wall is a large tub of manure. Hanging on the walls near the door are various garden tools.

Rotting wooden tables line the side walls. On the tables are an assortment of clay flower pots and some small envelopes of onion and radish seeds. Half the pots are empty and half have dirt in them. One of the flower pots (on the left rear table) is larger and more ornate than the others. Close examination reveals these words inlaid in the pot:

I ride the wind, I sail the sea,
I travel underground.
I nest in bird and fish and tree --
In everything I'm found.

Sometimes I sink into a hole
And wind up stranded there
But soon I overrun the bowl
Or take again to air.

I sneak into the smallest crack
To split a stone in twain.
Without a top or front or back
I never can be slain!

So place me all around the floor,
You won't believe your eyes.
Or turn around, go through the door,
And so forego your prize.

Dungeon Designer Information

The answer to the riddle is *water*. To solve this room the players must sprinkle water all over the floor. In the room amongst the gravel and rubble is a `Jack and the Beanstalk' magic seed. When the seed is touched by water, it will sprout a thick, easy to climb stalk that shoots upwards. The beanstalk will break through the ceiling, climbing 100 feet in the air. Fifty feet above this room is a small alcove containing the treasure. At the top of the beanstalk you may also place a door leading to more of your dungeon.

<u>Treasure</u>

Three Magic Beans	These beans are just like the magic bean in the room. When watered, they will send a stalk 100 feet into the air.
Ever-full canteen	Holds 1 gallon of water, refills itself every hour.
Scroll of water walking	This spells allows the caster to walk on water for 1 hour

<u>Players Need</u>

Water

The players have discovered a well. An inscription on the bucket reads:

More valued than gold, more precious than silk
Pouring like wine, flowing like milk.
A count's nightly feast, an offering of war,
A pact is now sealed, forever more.

Dungeon Designer Information

The answer to the riddle is *blood.* To solve this room, each player must put a drop of his blood into the well and make a small wish. When a player does this, the water in the well will cloud over, and suddenly appear to be a window, showing the player whatever he has wished for. The player may then reach into the well and actually grab the item.

Each player may make only one minor wish. If a player offers something to the well other than blood (for example, throws in a copper piece) his wish will not be granted.

Treasure

Minor Wishes

Players who wish for reasonable items will be able to pull them from the well. Players who wish for large or extravagant items will either get something similar or perhaps a map which could lead them to their wish.

Dilemma #6

Hall of Flame

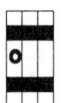

The door is made of heavy stone and slightly warm to the touch. On it is written (in mirror image)

A nasty little maze have we
To hurt you on your way
Ignore the things that you can see
And do just what I say

Turn left and step, then one step more,
Then pivot to the right,
Step once, then twice, turn left, move four
Your goal is now in sight.

Turn left again and step just twice,
You're there without a doubt!
Turn right and step and in a trice,
You're safely headed out.

A nasty little maze have we
To hurt you on your way
Ignore the things that you can see
And do just what I say

Turn left and step, then one step more,
Then pivot to the right,
Step once, then twice, turn left, move four
Your goal is now in sight.

Turn left again and step just twice,
You're there without a doubt!
Turn right and step and in a trice,
You're safely headed out.

When you open the door, you see that the floor is made up of red square paving stones. From all of the stones except the one directly in front of you, searing flames shoot up to the ceiling.

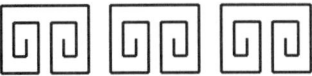

Dungeon Designer Information

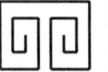

This is indeed a nasty little maze. The players can safely step on the open tile, but after that they must brave the flames. Luckily, many of the flames are part of a powerful illusion. The poem on the door gives the players the information they need to solve this maze. However, like the poem, the players must do everything in mirror image (i.e. left becomes right and vice versa). Therefore, to get safely through the maze, from the safe square the players must:

1. Turn right. Step three squares.
2. Turn left. Step three squares.
3. Turn right. Step four squares.
4. Turn right. Step two squares.
5. Turn left. Their next step takes them out of the maze.

The map on the next page shows which squares have real flame (shaded) and which have illusionary flame (clear).

The players start the maze in square G1, facing square G2. They exit the room by going out of M2, which will be to their left when they arrive there. You'll notice that the players' map does not show either the exit door or which squares have illusionary flames. As far as they can tell, every square but G1 has flames roaring up to the ceiling. The door out of M2 cannot be seen until a player enters that square.

When the players go left out of M2 they will be in a 10' x 10' room which has the treasure and a door leading into a new part of your dungeon.

Obstacles

Flames: The whole room is ensorcelled by a powerful illusion. It will be impossible for players to tell real flames from illusionary ones without stepping into the square. Any inanimate object placed into a square will burn whether the square has real flame or not. If a player touches a real flame he will take moderate damage. A player who tries to walk into a square with real flame will also take moderate damage, but he will be unable to actually enter the square due to the intense heat.

Treasure

Amulet of protection from flames

The wearer of this amulet can withstand any normal fire, and takes only 1/4 damage from magical fire.

Fire Sword

The sword can cut through ice, and does double normal damage to cold-dwelling creatures.

Wand of fireballs

This wand shoots small fireballs which will hit one target doing moderate damage.

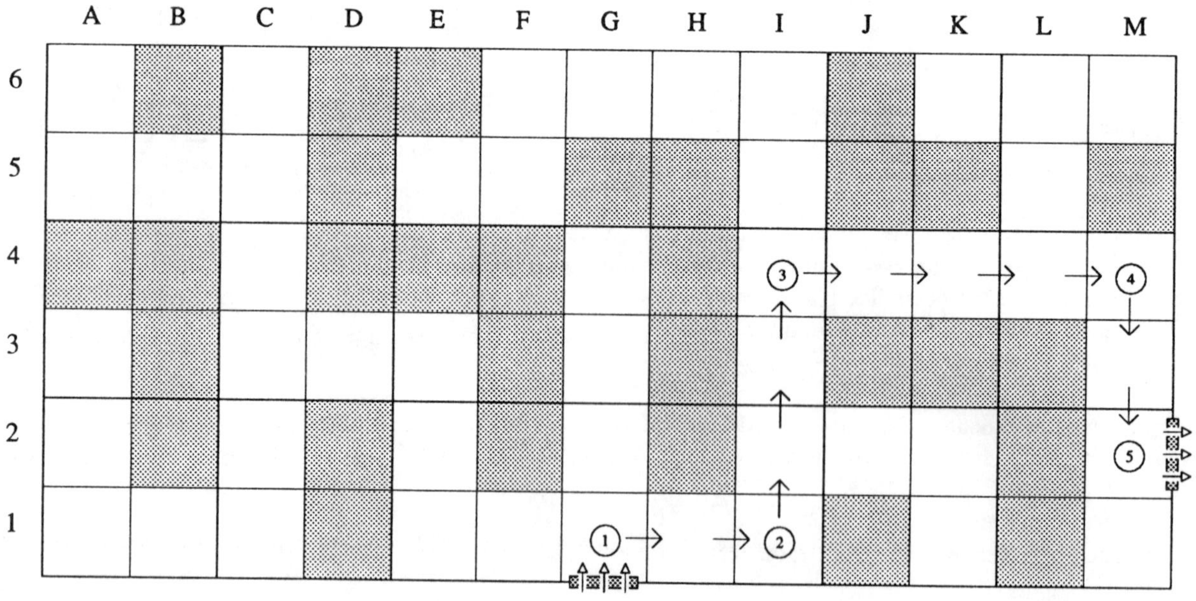

Shaded areas are real flame
Clear areas are illusionary flames

Dilemma #7

Grandma's Sitting Room

This is a sitting room filled with knick-knacks and bric-a-brac. The furniture consists of a couch, table, stool and desk. On shelves around the room are flowers (rose, tulip, daffodil, marigold and snapdragon), beverages (wine, mead, apple juice and water), paintings (ocean scene, still life, and portrait of an elderly woman), small ivory figurines (cat, dog, fox, lamb, pig, pony, raven and wolf), a collection of broken spoons (silver, gold, brass and jade) and books (dictionary, novel and picture book of dragons). On the wall is a faded tapestry which says:

It prods a man's hand, and it robs him of sleep,
It makes him climb mountains and travel the deep,
It makes him go wander down deep in a cave,
And do almost anything, stupid or brave.
The longer denied, the greater it grows,
It makes a man learn till he thinks that he knows.

Dungeon Designer Information

The solution to this riddle is *curiosity*. To solve this room the players must recall the expression "curiosity killed the cat" and destroy the cat figurine. Inside the cat is a tiny scroll which reads:

(Give the players Illustration #7-A)

Use my beasties carefully
And very happy you will be.
Call them by their rightful name
Or none of them will be quite tame.

Break the beasties one by one --
They'll each come back when each is done.
If the beasties go awry
Broken they might stay and die.

Felix Sheep and Winsome Dog
Minxy Fox and Lovely Hog
Raven Fast and Sleepy Horse
And Lastly Cunning Wolf Of Course.

<u>Special Treasure</u>

Magic Animal Figurines

If not broken, each is worth ten times the value of an ounce of ivory. However, as indicated by the scroll, these are magic figurines and their true worth is in their powers. If a figurine is called by its rightful name and then broken, it will come to life, perform one task, and then turn back into a figurine. However, there are warnings given in the poem which must be heeded:

To correctly invoke an animal, a player must call out its *full* name as given in the poem. For example, to get the lamb you must say `Felix Sheep', not just `Felix' or `Sheep'.

If an animal is invoked with the wrong name, or only part of its full name, it will start shimmering into existence then fade back into a figurine. Each time this happens the figurine has a 50% chance of shattering. If a figurine is broken without invocation the animal is gone forever.

Only one figurine can be animated at a time. Any figurine invoked while another is animated shatters, and animals that are killed while animated do not come back as figurines.

The animals and their abilities are:

Animal	Name	Ability
dog	Winsome Dog	Guard Dog.
fox	Minxy Fox	Climb, fetch things from small places.
pony	Sleepy Horse	A slow but strong horse.
lamb	Felix Sheep	Warm any who huddle against it.
raven	Raven Fast	Fly, carry messages, speak, scout.
pig	Lovely Hog	Excellent tracking by smell.
wolf	Lastly Cunning Wolf of Course	Combat.

For combat, you should assign appropriate combat abilities depending on your system. With the exception of Lastly Cunning Wolf of Course, most of the animals are not very useful in combat.

At the Buzzer

Dilemma #8

This small crawlway is blocked by several pieces of wood leaning against it. Around the edges, several bees have crawled out, and if you look inside, you can see a small cave filled with a swarm of bees. Written on the wood is:

An ebon spirit rises high
Child of air and fire
Born in death yet by wind borne
It flies but does not tire

It takes your life without a wound
Of that you can be sure
And though it claws into your eyes
It too may also cure.

Dungeon Designer Information

The answer to the riddle is *smoke* (the last line refers to using smoke to cure meats). To solve this Dilemma the players must create a large amount of smoke. This will drive the bees out through a small crack in the ceiling. With the bees gone, the treasure will be in plain view in a niche inside the cave.

Anything else the players do may have some effect but will not drive off or kill enough bees to allow the players to locate the treasure. A fireball will fry zillions of the bees, but more will quickly appear. Likewise, wind will push the bees back for a few seconds but they will soon adjust.

Players who examine the riddle may notice that it was written in charcoal.

Monsters

Bees — If the players decide to enter the room without getting rid of the bees, they will be unable to see clearly and will be constantly stung, causing minor damage.

Treasure

Magic Cornucopia

This can create either flowers or honey on demand.

Magic insect repellent

Will protect the players from insects or from monsters that are closely related to insects.

Magic amber

This piece of amber has a small bee inside. If the amber is broken, the bee will turn into a giant bee which a player can ride. The bee will also aid the player in combat, stinging opponents and causing them temporary paralysis.

Players Need

Ability to start a fire or create smoke. Note that the wood which the riddle is written on will smoke nicely if burnt.

Dilemma #9

Perfect Harmony

Scattered about this room are a number of battered musical instruments. Cymbals, drums, flutes, pipes and other instruments litter the floor. A dented gong hangs from the ceiling. Nearby, a harp with broken strings rests in the dust. A table holds several cracked ceramic bells, all with flaking wooden handles. The conductor's stand holds a broken baton and a piece of paper which reads:

While separately each of us breaks
Together we can make a stand.
Entwined like countless tangled snakes
We form a strong, yet supple band.

Now call me by my rightful name
And tell me what to do.
Together we shall win great fame
And massive fortunes too!

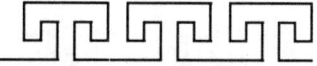

Dungeon Designer Information

The answer to the riddle is *rope*. To solve this room the players must give the rope (which attaches the gong to the ceiling) commands to follow. For example, saying "Rope, untie" will cause the rope to untie from both the ceiling and gong, making the gong fall to the floor.

Special Treasure

Magic Rope.

The rope obeys the following commands:

Rope, Climb The rope will climb virtually any surface. If held firmly at the base it will even climb straight up through the air like a magician's climbing rope trick.

Rope, Crawl Similar to "climb" except the rope crawls along the ground.

Rope, Lengthen The rope will lengthen to as much as 500 feet. The rope will also obey "longer."

Rope, Shorten The rope will shorten to as little as 5 feet. It grows skinnier as it does so until it looks like twine. The rope will also obey "shorter" and "shrink."

Rope, Tie The rope will tie itself firmly to anything nearby to which a rope can normally be tied. The knot cannot be untied except by using the untie command (below). The rope will also obey "knot."

Rope, Untie The rope will untie itself. It will also obey "unknot" or "loosen".

For example:

Rope, climb up that cliff.
Rope, crawl across the bridge.
Rope, tie to that tree.

The rope is very strong (able to hold about 1000 pounds) and is very hard to cut.

Dead Men Tell No Tales

Dilemma #10

The heavy, iron door to this room has been blocked by the partial collapse of the ceiling. It's a fairly simple job to unblock the door from the outside, but it's obvious that nobody inside the room could have forced the door open.

Inside this 20' square room are four skeletons. Two in the corner closest to the door are in pitted and dented armor and obviously died violent deaths (one beheaded, the other stabbed). The other two skeletons, wearing only robes, show no signs of physical damage. In the bony fingers of one of these is a scrap of yellowed parchment on which, written in dried blood, are the words:

I lie here defeated, my life slips away,
Though I used to conquer this foe every day,
My killer's relentless, and touches me now,
I know he'll succeed, but to you I vow,
Give me the weapon, after I've died,
I'll breathe once again, and tell you what I spied.

Dungeon Designer Information

The two robed skeletons died of *hunger* after they were trapped in the room. The two in armor went crazy when they discovered they were trapped and slew each other, leaving the other two to starve to death. To solve this room a player must put food in the skeleton's hand or mouth. When they do, the skeleton will animate and tell the players that before they died, the two who starved hid all their valuables in a secret compartment (undetectable by other means) in the wall opposite the door. The skeleton will tell the players how to find and open the compartment.

Treasure

A Treasure Map

The Skeleton's Treasure

Being dead, the skeleton no longer has use for money or gems and will gladly give the players his valuables.

The Skeleton

Giving the skeleton food will bring him back to life to complete a task which was left unfinished when he died. He will offer to help the players on their adventure in return for their help on his mission. This could act as a starting point to a whole new part of your campaign.

Players Need

Food

Dilemma #11

Hidden Tomb

The door to this 15' x 25' room blends in with the surrounding walls making it very difficult to notice. As you slide the door open, you are hit by a blast of cold, stale air. The side walls of the room are coated with ice. On the back of the door is a shattered mirror in a red frame, with pieces of the mirror lying on the floor just inside. The room contains five stone sarcophagi (coffins). Each sarcophagus is adorned by a small gem and a painted symbol, and each contains a skeleton. Each skeleton is uniquely attired. The crypt's contents are:

	Crypt 1	Crypt 2	Crypt 3	Crypt 4	Crypt 5
Gem:	Diamond	Ruby	Emerald	Sapphire	Topaz
Symbol:	Rearing Horse	Crescent Moon	Red Rose	Red Wine	Tiger
Attire:	Chain Mail	Gray Robes	Green Dress	Butler's Attire	Red Dress with Veil

In the center of the room on a black table is a scroll which gives off a faint light. Written on the scroll is:

Entrapped within a hidden tomb
With walls of bloodied ice
A maiden sleeps in scarlet gloom
And pays an awful price.

While flame can never hurt these walls
Your life may hold the key.
A gentle warmth can melt the walls
And set the maiden free.

Now find yourself a virgin knife
That's warmed by body heat
And spill the crimson of your life
And coat the walls complete.

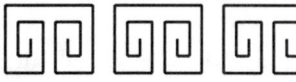

Dungeon Designer Information

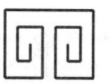

The true hidden tomb in this room is the ruby in the second crypt. All of the gems here are valuable, but the ruby has a noticeable flaw. Close examination of the flaw will reveal that it is actually a tiny maiden sleeping within the ruby.

To free the maiden the players must find a "virgin knife" - a sharp object that has never spilt blood (for example a shard from the mirror). One of the players must warm it with his body heat, then cut himself and coat the ruby with blood. When this has been done, the ruby will shatter and the maiden will revert to her normal size.

The Maiden

The maiden can lead the players on to new adventures. For example she could be a wealthy heiress who was imprisoned many years ago by an evil wizard. She now seeks to reclaim her birthright. Or she could be a powerful wizard who will help the players on their quest. She could even fall in love with one of the players.

Treasure

Gems

In addition to the Ruby, the players can also remove the Diamond, Emerald, Sapphire and Topaz. The gems are small but valuable.

Knight Riders

Dilemma #12

Dungeon Designer: If your players do not know how to play chess, skip this room. They need not be good but they must know how all the pieces move. Also if you do not know how the chess pieces move, either get a player to take over for you during this room or skip it. If you have a chess set, you should set up the room with it.

On the outside of the door to this room are the following words:

> Move like a Knight, you'll be all right
> But use the greatest care
> To plan it all and never fall
> Upon a guarded square.

Dungeon Designer Information

The room inside's floor is a giant chess board. There are several six foot tall white chess pieces on the board in the positions shown on the map. White's King stands in front of the only other door in the room.

On the square in front of you is a large black stone horse. The enormous saddle can carry everyone in the party. The horse says "Please be mounted".

To solve this room the players must mount the horse and cross the room by moving like a Knight does in chess. They must capture the White King and then exit through the far door.

The only way for players to move about this room is to mount the black horse. Once mounted, the horse will say "Please tell me where to move". The horse will only move like a Knight. The players will not be able to dismount except to exit through one of the doors.

If the players end on a square that is protected by a white chess piece, a force beam shoots out of the protecting piece and knocks them back to their previous position doing moderate damage to each rider.

If the players land on a white chess piece which is *not* protected by another white piece, the captured piece shrinks into a small, crystal chess piece, as valuable as small diamond. The horse will scoop the crystal piece up with its mouth and present it to the players. That piece is then out of the chess game.

Because of the way in which the white pieces protect each other, the players will not be able to move directly to the door. The King is protected by a Bishop so the players must capture the bishop first. It is not easy to get safely to the Bishop however, so the players will need to capture other pieces first. The map on the next page shows one possible solution but any legal solution should be allowed. The numbers indicate the order of moves the player should make. Your players may find another solution.

Monsters

Chess Pieces

These pieces shoot forces beams which cannot be countered. The white chess pieces never move.

Treasure

Crystal Chess Pieces

Once a captured piece is turned to crystal, it's worth about as much as a small diamond.

Black and White Pearl Chess Board

If the players capture all the pieces on the board except the other knights, upon exiting the room they will find a valuable chess board made from black and white pearls.

The King

When the players capture the White King, instead of immediately turning to crystal, he will shimmer and turn into a real human King. This King will commend the players for their skill and bravery, and will knight each player in the group. This will bestow on each player either a minor special ability or aid them in gaining Levels. The King will then take the black horse and ride off.

OUR SOLUTION

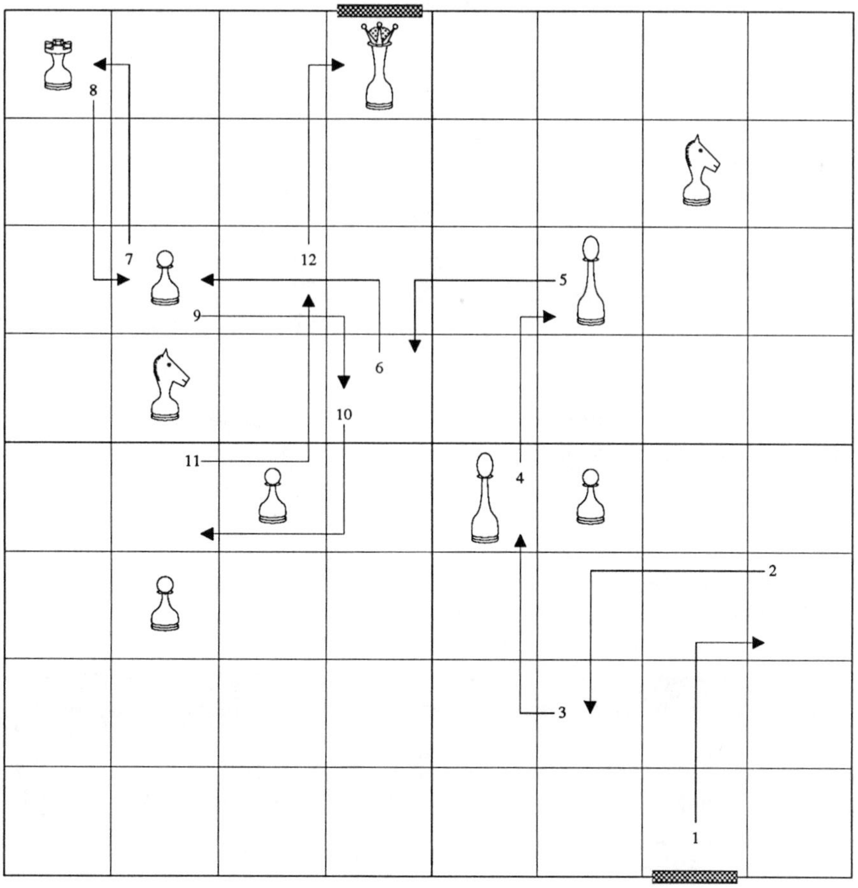

Warriors, Wyverns and Rocs

Dilemma #13

In the center of this room is a large stone table with two ornate chairs. On the walls of the room are several paintings showing:

Wyvern	A huge Wyvern stands alone. Below him is a glimmering scroll.
Warrior	A tired warrior rests with a rune-covered sword.
Tree	A huge tree with a giant nest. In the nest, looking like a giant egg, is a strange gem.

The paintings are fairly dark, almost as if the sun had recently set in each of them.

Carved into the top of the table are the words:

I often have leaves, though I'm not a tree,
Sharp knives all around, I never do flee,
For though I'm often surrounded, I never feel fear,
And a good turn in time, makes treasure appear!

Dungeon Designer Information

The answer to the riddle is *table*. To solve this room the players must turn the table. The table is fairly heavy, but can be turned slowly by a single person, or quickly by several. When the table is turned, a secret panel (not detectable by other means) will slide back under the table. Beneath it is a small cavity where the room's treasure lies.

The paintings are traps, and if turned, the scene in that painting will change:

Wyvern	The Wyvern will laugh and say "Foolish mortals! So easily confused by my tricks!" He will then breathe flame, incinerating the *Moon Scroll.*
Warrior	The tired warrior will dejectedly shake his head and say "You must be more careful. Heed the riddle!". He will then turn and walk away with the *Twilight Sword.*
Tree	A Roc will fly into the picture, grab the *Sunset Gem* and fly away screeching "Bird brains! Trying to steal my treasure!".

Each painting will change only once. If it is turned again, the painting will not change. Once a treasure has disappeared from a painting, it also disappears from the hidden compartment under the table.

<u>Treasure</u>

Twilight Sword	During the day this sword does only half normal damage. However, at night, it does double normal damage, and during the hour the sun is setting, does triple normal damage.
Sunset Gem	During the day, this appears to be a lump of coal, but at sunset, it will turn into a valuable gem of the player's choice (diamond, ruby, emerald, etc.). At dawn, it will revert to looking like coal.
Moon Scroll	A magician may transfer any one spell he knows to this scroll. This spell can then be cast by a non-magic user from the Moon Scroll during any full moon. Once the spell is cast, the Moon Scroll becomes blank again and may be reused.

Vanity

In this room the players find a broken down old bed (not pictured), a chair and a chest of drawers (a vanity) with a large mirror on top. On the vanity is a jewelry box. Inscribed in the top of the jewelry box is a poem:

,htaerb latrom htiw gof ot nrut I	*I turn to fog with mortal breath,*
htaed sa llits sa dnop a ekil rO	*Or like a pond as still as death*
erac ohw esoht ot llet syawla I	*I always tell to those who care*
riaf tey ohw dna ylgu si ohW	*Who is ugly and who yet fair*
,oot ,wonk dluohs uoy gniht eno s'erehT	*There's one thing you should know, too,*
.uoy ta kool uoy em ta kool uoy nehW	*When you look at me you look at you.*

There is nothing valuable in or around the bed, and the drawers are empty except for an old mouse nest.

When you open the jewelry box it plays a tune and reveals three wooden boxes: one labeled ƧMƎG which contains bits of broken glass, one labeled ЯƎV⅃IƧ with small scraps of tin and one labeled ᗡ⅃OG with small beads of brass.

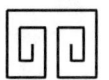

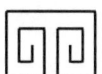

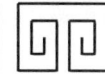

Dungeon Designer Information

The answer to the riddle is *mirror* and the mirror plays a key part. The mirror is magical, and has the following properties:

- It cannot be moved or broken
- Anything touching the glass will pass through to the other side
- Any object passing through the mirror will become its mirror image on the other side
- Anyone looking at the mirror will see what they would see in an ordinary mirror. The mirror does not show the room on the other side. So if a person walks through the mirror he will seem to disappear from the bedroom.

To solve this room, the players must walk or reach through the mirror and take the boxes from that room. When they return through the mirror the boxes will read (and contain) GEMS, SILVER and GOLD.

The room on the other side of the mirror is a mirror image of the bedroom. It contains mirror images of the items that started in the bedroom. The exceptions to this are the boxes in the jewelry box. The ones in the mirror room also read ƧMƎG, ЯƎV⅃IƧ, and ᗡ⅃OG. The mirror room has no exits except the mirror.

If the boxes from the bedroom are carried into the mirror room, they will transform into GEMS, SILVER and GOLD. When carried back through the mirror, they again become ƧMƎG, ЯƎV⅃IƧ, and ᗡ⅃OG. When the boxes from the *mirror room* are carried back into the bedroom, they become GEMS, SILVER and GOLD.

Treasure

Gems, Silver and Gold

Jewelry Boxes

The Jewelry Boxes in both the bedroom and the mirror room are valuable because they are intricately carved and play music.

Doorways to Danger

Dilemma #15

On the other side of the room are three doors. In the middle of the room is a pedestal on which rests a red key, a green key, and a blue key. Examining the keys you see fine writing on them:

<u>Red key</u>
I am the key to set you free,
The Blue will only lie.
Now set your sight upon the right
And off you all can fly.

<u>Green key</u>
The Blue's the key although, you see,
It has no truth to say,
That you should chose and quickly use
To go the middle way.

<u>Blue key</u>
I am a key that you should flee
Just use the one that lies.
If you go left, you'll be bereft
And maybe someone dies.

Carved on the pedestal itself is more writing which says:

Red and Green and sapphire Blue --
Only one will tell you true.
One will lead to pain and fears
Feeding lies into your ears.
One gives both the bad and good
Still they can be understood.
Think before you reach and choose;
Always know you've much to lose.
Think before you reach and choose --
Always know you've much to lose.

Dungeon Designer Information

To solve this puzzle the players must determine which key always tells the truth, which key always lies, and which "gives both the bad and good." To do this, assume each key in turn tells the truth, and see for which keys this leads to a contradiction. You will find that the Blue key tells the truth, the Green key always lies, and the Red tells some truths and some lies. The Blue key says to use the Green key to get out. The Red key tells some lies and some truths. Since the first two statements made by the Red are lies, the third statement, to use the Right door, must be true. So to exit the room, the players should open the Right door with the Green key.

If a player attempts any combination other than the Right door and the Green key, as soon as the key is placed in the door, a lightening bolt will come out of the lock, permanently fusing the key into the door, and doing moderate damage to the player.

When the players open the Right hand door with the Green key, they will find treasure and a passage leading to more of the dungeon.

<u>Treasure</u>

Three Keys	When taken from the room become made from Ruby, Emerald and Sapphire
Magic Skeleton Key	80% chance of opening any locked door
Minor Genie	He will answer three simple questions truthfully

Dilemma #16

Scared Senseless

The floor of this room is tiled in large hexes at varying heights. They range in height from six feet above ground level to six feet below. The entry square is at ground level and has a poem inscribed into it:

The mirrors of your soul will say
That there is nothing here.
Your tongue will also tell you nay
As will the sharpest ear.

Your fingers pass right through my skin --
There's nothing here to feel.
But find me now and stand within
And quickly you will heal.

Dungeon Designer Information

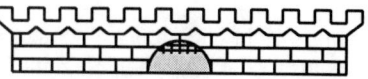

The poem indicates that the players will not be able to detect the object in question using sight (the eyes are the "mirrors of the soul"), taste, hearing, or touch. The only one of the five senses not mentioned is smell.

To find the treasure the players must sniff the air in the room. They will detect a faint almond odor. If they try to follow the smell, it will move away from them. If the players work together to surround and corner the smell, they will succeed fairly easily.

The smell is generated by an invisible cloud of gas. Any player standing within the cloud will heal up to full strength. Once a player has been healed, he becomes immune to the gas and cannot use it again.

A fully healed player who stands in the gas will get a permanent increase in an appropriate statistic (depending on your role playing system).

Special Treasure

Healing.

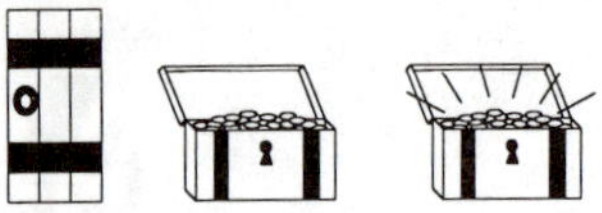

Wizard's Workshop

Dilemma #17

The door to this 15' x 20' room is locked yet can be easily opened with a key hanging nearby. Inside you see what seems to be an alchemist's workshop.

Just inside the door is a human skeleton. Along the right wall stands a large bookcase with a few dozen books on various magical topics. They crumble when touched and are not worth much. In a cabinet to the left are jars containing honey, water and algae. Atop the cabinet is an old scale.

Along the left wall is a work bench on which lies a crucible, several glass beakers, a small lead bar, parts of skeletons from several animals including two huge vertebrae from some dragon-sized animal, metal tongs, and an open book. Most of the pages are unreadable. The book is open to a page which says:

I am that which will never rust,
Between friends will erode trust,
Sunlight caught inside your hand,
Maker of Kings, destroyer of land,

From lead it comes, instead of mine,
By a secret hidden in the spine.

In the right rear corner is a small stone furnace and a full box of coal. Next to the far wall is a full-sized iron statue of a king. He holds a raised sword in his right hand and he holds his left hand outstretched.

Carved on the wall behind the statue is:

My patience is ended, my mystical friend,
You now must deliver, no longer pretend,
Here you shall stay, no longer free,
Until what you promised, you yield unto me.

Dungeon Designer Information

The answer to the riddle in the book is *gold.* The poem by the statue explains the alchemist's situation. He told his patron he would create gold from lead and, when he failed to produce results, the king had him sealed in this chamber. To solve this room, the players must place gold in the statue's outstretched hand.

If the players do this, a secret door (undetectable by any other means) will open behind the statue. This door opens on a passage which leads to the alchemist's quarters where the players will find some worthless furniture: a bed, wardrobe and table. Inside the wardrobe is a pile of rotten clothing, under which is the treasure. The room can also have a door leading to another section of your dungeon.

However, there is more to be gained from this room than the alchemist's belongings. He had all of the ingredients needed to create gold from lead, but couldn't figure out how. The last lines in the book:

> From lead it comes instead of mine
> By a secret hidden in the spine

hold the key. The spine refers to the spine of the book and if the players look there or take the book apart, they will discover a small scroll.

The scroll reads:

(Give the players Illustration #17-A)

> **Grind the dragon marrow well,**
> **Add some honey, make it gel.**
> **Sift the coal and lead on top,**
> **Mix five minutes without a stop.**
> **Magically bake for half an hour -**
> **Shiny yellow starts to flower.**

If the players make the concoction and place it in the furnace, in a half hour they will have a moderate amount of gold.

The furnace in the room is magical, and anything placed inside of it will heat up very quickly. Anyone putting his hand in the furnace will take minor damage from the heat. The furnace is molded from the same stone as the floor and hence cannot be moved.

<u>Monster</u>

Animated Statue

If the players touch the statue, or place anything in its hand except gold the statue will animate and attack everything that moves for five rounds doing minor damage each round. The statue fights like an experienced fighter and is unkillable. After five rounds it returns to its original position.

<u>Treasure</u>

Alchemist's belongings

The Alchemist had a small amount of silver and a minor potion.

Gold

Made by the players from the spell.

Spell

For creating gold from lead.

Pendants

Dilemma #18

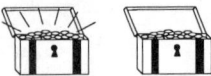

You climb a ladder down into a large rough-hewn chamber with seven doors, each leading to an alcove. Each alcove is different:

<u>(Clockwise from the top)</u>

Alcove 1:	A hardened crystal moon embedded high in the rock wall. Inside the crystal is a pouch.
Alcove 2:	Complete Darkness. No light (even magical) can penetrate the gloom.
Alcove 3:	20' wide chasm. On the other side is a small box.
Alcove 4:	A complex maze.
Alcove 5:	A deep, dark pit. The bottom of the pit can't be seen.
Alcove 6:	A sheer wall with a high ledge at the top.
Alcove 7:	Long corridor. The air is unbreathable. The end is not in sight.

On a stalagmite in the center of the room is a velvet lined box. Inside the box are eight pendants, each in the shape of an animal: Bat, Frog, Giraffe, Rat, Raven, Spider, Whale, Wolf. As you examine the box, the Raven pendant suddenly speaks:

A different helper, one per door,
You can use each once, then Nevermore!

Dungeon Designer Information

To solve this room, the players must wear the correct amulet in each of the seven alcoves. Each amulet will confer one natural ability of the animal to the player wearing it. For example, a player wearing the bat pendant could fly or have sonar. Each pendant can only be worn once, and only one ability can be gained. This ability will be lost again once the player has used it in an alcove. The pendants do not work outside of this room unless the players solve all seven alcoves (see *Treasure*). The Raven pendant has no ability other than speaking the above rhyme.

Conventional means to solve the challenges presented in the alcoves will always fail. For example, a player with jumping ability will feel heavy and be unable to jump the chasm. The challenges can only be overcome by using an appropriate animal pendant in each alcove. When a player puts on an amulet, ask which ability of that animal he is going to use. Note that some pendants can solve more than one alcove, but there is only one combination which solves all seven alcoves. The correct solution is:

Alcove 1:	use Wolf to howl and shatter the crystal moon.
Alcove 2:	use Bat to gain sonar or exceptional hearing to find the treasure.
Alcove 3:	use Frog to jump chasm.
Alcove 4:	use Rat to learn the maze or smell the treasure at the end of the maze.
Alcove 5:	use Spider to weave a thread to descend the pit.
Alcove 6:	use Giraffe to gain long neck and reach a pouch.
Alcove 7:	use Whale to hold breath all the way down the corridor.

Alternate ways of solving individual rooms are:

Alcove 3:	use Bat to fly and get box.
Alcove 6:	use Bat to fly up and get pouch, or use Spider to climb wall and get pouch

<u>Treasure</u>

Each of the seven alcoves may contain some valuables (gold, gems, etc.)

Animal Pendants

If all the alcoves are solved the pendants will begin to glow. The pendants can then be used outside of this room. Each pendant can be used once per day.

Dilemma #19

Crypt of Charon

Dungeon Designer's Note: This room requires that your players have some knowledge of mythology. In mythology, Charon was the ferry-man who took the souls of the dead across the river Styx into the next world. The toll for passage was paid by placing a copper coin on each of the dead person's eyes.

\------

In the center of this hexagonal room is a six-sided altar carved from black stone on which lies what appears to be a fairly fresh corpse. Next to the table are two tall candles (which provide the only light in the room) and a large gong with a hammer.

Carved on the front of the altar are the words:

Find the key 'ere the Darkness is filled.
Empty, yet waiting for when Life is stilled.
Enter and rest, with Charon's toll
Held fast and sure to the Windows of the Soul.
Sound the gong in the dead of the night.
Be wary, stray not, on your Stygian flight.
Take only that to which Earth belong
'Ere the Shadow o'er all begin his Dark Song.
Once only you may try to go free with one Goal.
Else hapless you'll roam in the Pit of Sheol.

There is a metal statue in each corner of the room. Although the candle light barely reaches the statues, you can see that the statues are all human and each carries a different item. Clockwise from the door they are:

- Chain mail and halberd
- Plate armor and broadsword
- Bear skin and axe
- Robes and staff
- Chain mail and loaded crossbow
- Black leather and garrote

In the middle of each of the six walls except the one with the door is a 2' x 3' plaque made of the same black stone as the altar.

Dungeon Designer Information

The corpse on the altar died from wounds that seem to have been inflicted by the statues. She had a small dagger and a pouch containing a few gold, silver coins and a dozen coppers.

If the players experiment with the plaques, they will discover that these are the blank fronts of crypts. They can all be easily slid out of the wall and all are empty.

Each minute the players are in the room, the statues move a little closer to the center and the candles grow a little dimmer. After about ten minutes the statues will reach the edge of the altar and the candles will be completely out.

The poem relates to the custom of burying the dead with a coin on each eye. The coins were the toll charged by the ferryman Charon when he ferried the departed over the river Styx into the land of the dead.

The poem tells the players to lie in the crypts (or on the altar) with copper pieces on their eyes. When the "Darkness is filled" and the candles go completely out, a player must strike the gong. A player lying on the altar can easily reach the gong. Any players in the crypts or on the altar will then begin an astral journey.

If the players fail to strike the gong when the room is dark, each will be hit by one of the statues, doing minor damage. The statues will move back to their places, the candles will relight, and the room will become a regular crypt. The players will not be able to solve the room, even if they come back later.

Once the players enter the crypts and the gong is struck, tell them the following:

> **You are now floating on the river Styx atop your crypt (or altar). In the water are priceless objects of all kinds. You see chests overflowing with gems and jewels, potions, golden armor, weapons of power - just name it and it will float by shortly.**
>
> **You are rapidly approaching an island but you could probably grab one of the floating items first if you want to try.**

The riddle warns players to "stray not [in their] Stygian flight" and any player who tries to grab a floating item will fall out of their crypt and disappear from sight. When the astral journey is complete, that player will awake back in the room, having fallen out of his crypt onto the floor.

Once the players have reached the island, tell them:

> **Soon your odd craft land on the shore of a small island. Within a huge ring of fire to your right are many magnificent weapons and pieces of armor. Embedded in a large stone in front of you are priceless potions. At the bottom of a crystal clear pond on your left you can see hundreds of exquisite gems. Floating above your head are powerful magic scrolls.**

The players will find that any of the treasures on this island can be easily obtained. The fire does not burn, the potions can be easily pried from the stone, the water is shallow, and the scrolls can be plucked from the air. Each player may take whatever treasure he wants before getting back onto his crypt or altar. When a player reboards his crypt he instantly returns to the room. Any players on the river or island will see the player disappear.

However, the poem in the crypt warns the players:

> Take only that to which Earth belong
> 'Ere the Shadow o'er all begin his Dark Song.
> Once only you may try to go free with one Goal.
> Else hapless you'll roam in the Pit of Sheol.

The only treasures on this island which belongs to Earth are the potions (the weapons and armor belong to Fire, the gems to Water, and the scrolls to Air). Any player who tries to take something other than exactly one potion will find himself with no treasure at all when he returns to the crypt. A player who takes exactly one potion will have that potion when he returns.

<u>Treasure</u>

Any valuable potion.

Dilemma #20

Shadowman!

Dungeon Designer Note: Shadowman rooms are designed to be very challenging to your players. They are fun to play and extremely rewarding to solve, but by nature they put your players under a lot of pressure and can cause some frustration. The room contains everything needed to solve it, but players need to think creatively, and be willing to try various tactics in order to complete the room.

When you enter the room it looks like a large living room. However, as you open the door, you suddenly find all of your party in the room. When you recover, you notice that all of your possessions are gone, as are all of your abilities and spells. You are standing in the room, modestly clad in stylish loincloths (two piece models for the females).

The room contains the following obvious items (clockwise from the door) -

- A locked door through which you entered.
- A small rug nailed to the floor.
- A lightweight table with an oil lamp on it.
- A queen sized bed.
- A marble statue of a snake charmer.
- A glass case with a key inside.
- A small fountain containing fish, small plants, shells, and pebbles.
- A rusty suit of armor holding an extremely sharp battle axe.
- A small wooden chair.
- A cushioned chair.
- A small chest.

Hanging over the center of the room is:

- A glass chandelier suspended 40 feet off the floor by a chain bolted 13 feet from the floor.

> Suddenly a small, shadowy figure appears. He points at the door and says:
> There's just one way out
> But you can't get the key.
> There is treasure for you
> But the real fun's for me!

As quickly as he appeared, he is gone.

Dungeon Designer Information

The players have two goals in this room: (1) to escape Shadowman's house taking as little damage as possible and (2) to gain Shadowman's treasure.

Let the players puzzle a little bit over the room. Then choose a random player and tell him he feels like he's been stung, taking minor damage. The players will catch a brief glimpse of Shadowman flitting away from him.

This is the house of Shadowman, an annoying imp who lives mostly in two dimensions. His goal is to frustrate and torment the players but not to kill them. Each turn he will select a random player on whom to inflict minor damage. If any player gets close to death, Shadowman will say, "You're too weak to play with," toss the player out and relock the door all in the blink of an eye. The player's possessions are outside the door.

Shadowman moves at the speed of light and cannot be hurt by any means physical or magical.

Let each player perform one action per turn. For example, a player should be able to go to the glass case and try to open it in one turn. Only let the players spend about a minute deciding what to do next before their next turn. If they spend more than a minute before they tell you what they are going to do, Shadowman strikes!

To escape the room, the players will need to use the following items:

Locked door:	This is how the players leave. The key to the door is in the glass case.
Glass case:	The case is magically reinforced and can only be cut open with the diamond hidden in the chandelier. The key inside the case opens the door.
Chandelier:	Hidden inside the chandelier is a valuable diamond. It can be used to cut open the glass case. To get the diamond, the chain must be cut, making the chandelier drop to the floor. When the chandelier falls the glass will shatter into dust leaving only the diamond.
Chain:	Only players standing on the wooden chair can reach the chain. The table will not hold a player's weight and the chest is too small, but if the players have the magic carpet, that will work. If a player stands on the cushioned chair Shadowman will say, "Don't put foot prints on the cushions!" He will then yank the chair out from under the player. The chain can only be cut with the Battle Axe.
Wooden chair:	The players can stand on this chair to reach the chandelier.
Battle axe:	The axe is rusted to the suit of armor. The axe is used to cut down the chandelier.
Armor:	The armor must be oiled with the oil from the lamp to release its grip on the battle axe.
Oil lamp:	The oil in the lamp can be used to oil the armor to get the battle axe. The table it is on is ordinary and has no other use.

The other items in the room will give the players treasure:

Cushioned chair:	Any player searching the chair cushions will discover a rare coin of moderate value.
Bed:	If the nails from the rug are placed here it becomes a bed of nails.
Snake charmer:	If placed upon a bed of nails he will breathe a sigh of contentment, turn the carpet into a flying carpet for the players, and then return to immobility.
Rug:	The rug is nailed to the floor. The players can remove the nails with the hammer. Under the rug is a magical scroll.
Hammer:	The hammer is in the chest, and easily removes the nails holding the rug to the floor.
Chest:	The chest is unlocked and contains a hammer and a screwdriver.
Pond:	Among the shells at the bottom of the pond is an oyster.
Oyster:	To open the oyster, the players must use the screwdriver. Inside the oyster is a valuable black pearl. If the players try to take the oyster from the room without opening it, Shadowman will say, "You didn't earn that!" He will then slap the hand of the player carrying the oyster, doing minor damage, and will put the oyster back in the pond.
Screwdriver:	This is used to pry open the oyster.

If your players start getting frustrated you may want to give them some hints:

- **Everything you need to solve the room is in the room.**
- **Most everything in the room is important for either getting out or getting treasure.**
- **Most of the items need to interact with other things in the room.**

<u>Treasure</u>

Rare Coin	This coin is of moderate value.
Black Pearl	This pearl is of high value.
Magic Scroll	This is a moderately powerful scroll.
Magic Carpet	This flies as fast a horse can run and will carry up to 600 pounds.
Diamond	The diamond is of moderate value.
Battle Axe	This axe is of such high quality that it is as good as a magic axe.

Riddle Item

The Perilous Potion

You have acquired the remnants of an ancient booklet entitled *The Perilous Potion*. Who or what wrote it and what became of the rest of the book is unknown. Reading it you see it holds fourteen poems. What you do with this knowledge is up to you.

Poem #1
A drop of blood from tongueless one
Is how this potion is begun
Two bloodless ones of gold and red
A verdant soldier burned and dead
A prize still in the armor plate
That's kissed by soldier standing straight
Now sweeten this for hours three
Til more you look and less you see
Put four legs in, then let him go
And add an ace and stir it slow
Add last a bit of golden hair
And drink the mixture if you dare.
A potion good to make you strong.
A potion fell if aught is wrong.

Poem #2
As still as death with baited breath
He waits with lidless eye.
As cold as stone he waits alone
For prey to happen by.

And in a blink too quick to think
He strikes with lightening speed
And by and by the prey will die
And then it's time to feed.

Poem #3
A straight standing soldier
From his crest to his toe,
Combating all darkness,
His primary foe.
Though 'tis unfair
It's the profession he chose,
The longer he fights
The shorter he grows.

Poem #4
Time doth it sweeten, as it sweetens time,
Love it enhances it's skill is sublime,
Loosens the tongue as it quickens the heart,
Thieves, Saints, and Kings to each it plays part.

Poem #5
I guard my prize from squirrel fates
With sturdy armor all around
Until it's time to spread my plates
And drop my charges to the ground.

Poem #6
Upon my wings of rainbow lace
I soar upon the summer breeze
To hunt a noisome flying ace
Who stabs and drinks and spreads disease.

Poem #7
Just once a day I show my face
And once a day away I flee
And while I'm found without a chase
The more you look the less you see.

Poem #8
Within my veins no blood will flow
Yet I am quite alive.
I bask in Summer sunshine's glow
And for a while I thrive.

But when the chilly winds blow I,
Bedecked in gold and red,
Will tumble from my station high
And join the many dead.

Poem #9
Beneath the drowsy summer sun
I spread my golden hair.
From dawn until the day is done
I lie without a care.

My locks soon turn from gold to white
And so departs my ease.
My hair comes loose and takes to flight
Adrift upon the breeze.

Poem #10
In any weather we can thrive --
We flow across the plain,
And since we never are alive
We never can be slain.

Our presence you will never lack --
We never leave for long.
You chop us down -- we grow right back
An army thousands strong.

Poem #11
Our army marches 'cross the field
So thickly that we hide the dirt,
A million verdant blades we wield
Which cut but deal little hurt.

Poem #12
Legless runs beneath the trees
Tongueless murmurs to the breeze
Never sleeps within its bed
Cold as death but isn't dead.

Poem #13
First have no legs -- cannot swim,
Then grow one leg, fit and trim,
Soon enough I grow two more,
Next have five, then only four.

Poem #14
When red and orange fill the sky
And daylight's glow is fading,
I raise my bow and fiddle high
And start my serenading.

A single note is all I play,
The tempo's all I vary.
I'm somber on a chilly day
But when it's warm I'm merry.

DUNGEON DESIGNER INFORMATION

To give your players *The Perilous Potion* you need to remove the cover page and the three interior pages from the illustration tear outs. Fold all four pages along the center. Then insert the three interior pages inside the Perilous Potion cover. When you're done you'll have a 8½″ by 5½″ booklet.

Riddle Items are similar to Riddle Rooms but they aren't intended to be easily or quickly solved. Unlike a Riddle Room, the components needed to get the treasure are *not* supposed to be readily available. In a campaign setting it may take your players several game months to find all the ingredients.

The first poem describes how to mix The Perilous Potion and the remaining poems are riddles which the players must solve to find out what the potion ingredients are. To create the potion the players find the ingredients somewhere in your campaign and then mix them together as directed by the first poem. Each time the potion is mixed correctly it has a different power and one of the poems in the book disappears and is replaced by a the name of the potion created.

The answers to the riddles are: #2 – Snake*, #3 – Candle, #4 – Wine, #5 – Pine Cone, #6 – Dragonfly, #7 - Sunset, #8 – Leaf, #9 – Dandelion, #10 – Hair*, #11 – Grass, #12 – Stream or River, #13 – Frog or Toad, #14 – Cricket*.

* The Snake, Hair and Cricket answers are not used in mixing the potion.

The directions in the first poem tell the players to:

1) Start with a drop of fresh water (from Poem #12 - *Stream or River*)
2) Crumble in two leaves. Autumn leaves of red and gold will work the best (from Poem #8 - *Leaf*).
3) Add a burnt blade of grass (from Poem #11- *Grass*).
4) Singe a pine cone with a candle and toss it in (from Poems #5 - *Pine Cone* and #3 - *Candle*)
5) Soak the mixture in wine for three hours. The three hours must start before sunset and end while the sun is setting (from Poems #4 - *Wine* and #7 - *Sunset*).
6) Add a frog or toad. It must swim around in the potion for a time and then leave (from Poem #13 - *Frog or Toad*).
7) Add a mosquito (from Poem #6 - *Dragonfly*, although instead of adding a Dragonfly you add "the noisome ace" – the mosquito).
8) Add a few petals from a dandelion (from Poem #9 - *Dandelion*).
9) Drink the potion.

Each time the players mix the potion correctly, choose one of the fourteen poems. You may either roll a die or choose whichever potion seems most appropriate to your campaign at the time. Tell your players that the poem you selected disappears from the book and is replaced by the appropriate description below. Once a potion has been made, it can never be made again. Once all fourteen poems have been used up, *The Perilous Potion* book crumbles to dust.

If the players mix at least the first four ingredients properly, the magic of the book of *The Perilous Potion* is activated. If they make any mistakes after that point, the potion will explode doing moderate damage to those nearby. One of the remaining poems in the book will go blank at that point.

Poem	Description	What the potion does:
Poem #1	Peril or Prize	This is always the last poem to be activated. Choose any of the other powers, mix them together or give the potion whatever power you choose. All you tell the players is Peril or Prize.
Poem #2	Cure Poison	This potion will cure any poison.
Poem #3	Dark Sight	This gives the drinker the ability to see in the dark as clearly as if it were day. If one person drinks the entire potion, he receives this ability for life. It may be split up to eight ways with each dose lasting for a month.
Poem #4	Haste	The drinker can move up to five times his normal speed for five minutes.
Poem #5	Armor	This toughens the skin of the drinker providing defense equivalent to armor. If one person drinks the entire potion the effect lasts for life. It may be split up to eight ways with each dose lasting for a month.
Poem #6	Summon Dragonfly Mounts *Pour on the ground.*	Pouring a Summon Dragonfly potion on the ground will attract a swarm of dragonflies which will carry all players in the party who are no heavier than a normal human plus 50 pounds of equipment. The dragonflies will stay with the party until slain.
Poem #7	Flash *Throw at Enemies.*	When a container of this potion is thrown, it explodes on impact blinding all those facing that direction with open eyes. The blinding effect lasts for ten minutes.
Poem #8	Leaf Fall	This potion contains a dozen doses which allow a player to fall any distance without harm.
Poem #9	Cloud of Fuzz *Throw at Enemies.*	When a Cloud of Fuzz potion is thrown it will break on impact and fill a 20' x 20' x 10' high area with a swirling cloud of dandelion fuzz. Anyone within the cloud will be effectively blinded until the cloud dissipates (about ten minutes).
Poem #10	Entangle *Throw at Enemies.*	When even a single drop of this potion touches an opponent all his hair will rapidly grow and start to swirl and twist, entangling him in a trap of his own hair. The effect lasts for five minutes.
Poem #11	Blade Wall *Throw at Enemies.*	The Blade Wall potion creates a ten foot wide wall of small whirling blades. Anyone trying to pass through the barrier will take moderate damage.
Poem #12	Water Form	The drinker of a Water Form potion gains the ability to turn his body into water ten times. When in the Water Form a player can flow under doors and through cracks, is immune to attacks by most weapons, but must avoid fire and running or standing water. Getting within a few feet of either of these will cancel the spell.
Poem #13	Jump	The Jump potion allows the drinker to leap twenty feet horizontally or fifteen feet vertically. The potion contains twenty doses.
Poem #14	Warning	Drinking the Warning potion gives a player the permanent ability to detect ambushes. Traps or magic cannot be detected, only people or creatures lying in wait for an ambush or approaching.

Bonus Riddles

Bonus Riddles are provided for you to use to make up your own rooms, or to challenge your players with in other ways. For example, you could have your players encounter a Sphinx who will give treasure if the party can solve a riddle.

After the Riddle Room illustrations you'll find additional tear-out sheets with these riddles on them.

Bonus Riddle 1

A few have two, and many none,
A few have eight, but none have one,
The most have six, and lots have four,
A few have many, many more.

Bonus Riddle 2

Housed in crumbling temple, unseen by the eye,
Eternal and breathless, never to die.
It's said that I'm lost if your life's goal is greed,
Treasure's you've stored up that I'll never need.

Bonus Riddle 3

I'm never orange,
Though yellow can be.
A bard's good friend,
In his songs you find me.
In a child's book kept,
And in ballads too,
I'll bet you're surprised
Not to find me right here.

Bonus Riddle 4

Born of the union of water and sun,
A marvel of beauty if ever was one.
A cloak of majesty worn by the sky,
No one can touch it but all dreamers try.

Bonus Riddle 5

Without a mouth
Yet I can talk.
The mountains are my home,
Through the hills I walk,
Through the hills I,
Through the hills,
Through the,
Through!

Cover Riddle

I sleep by day and fly by night,
The moon hides me from mortal sight.
Reach for me but always fail.
Trust in me when you set sail.

Solutions to Bonus Riddles

1	**Legs**
2	**Soul**
3	**Rhyme**
4	**Rainbow**
5	**Echo**
cover	**Star**

Dilemma #1
Den of the Devourer

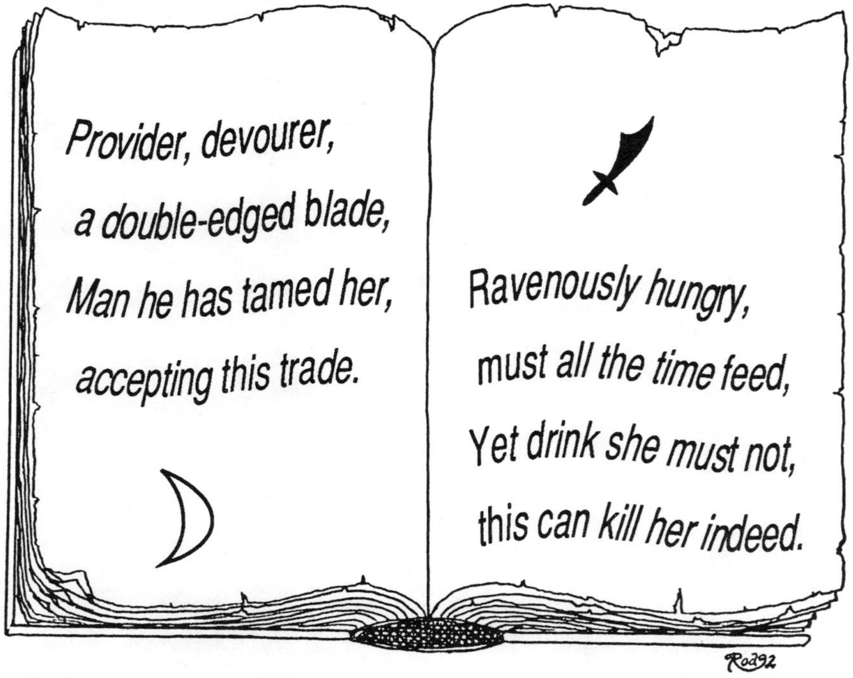

Provider, devourer,
a double-edged blade,
Man he has tamed her,
accepting this trade.
Ravenously hungry,
must all the time feed,
Yet drink she must not,
this can kill her indeed.
Rod92

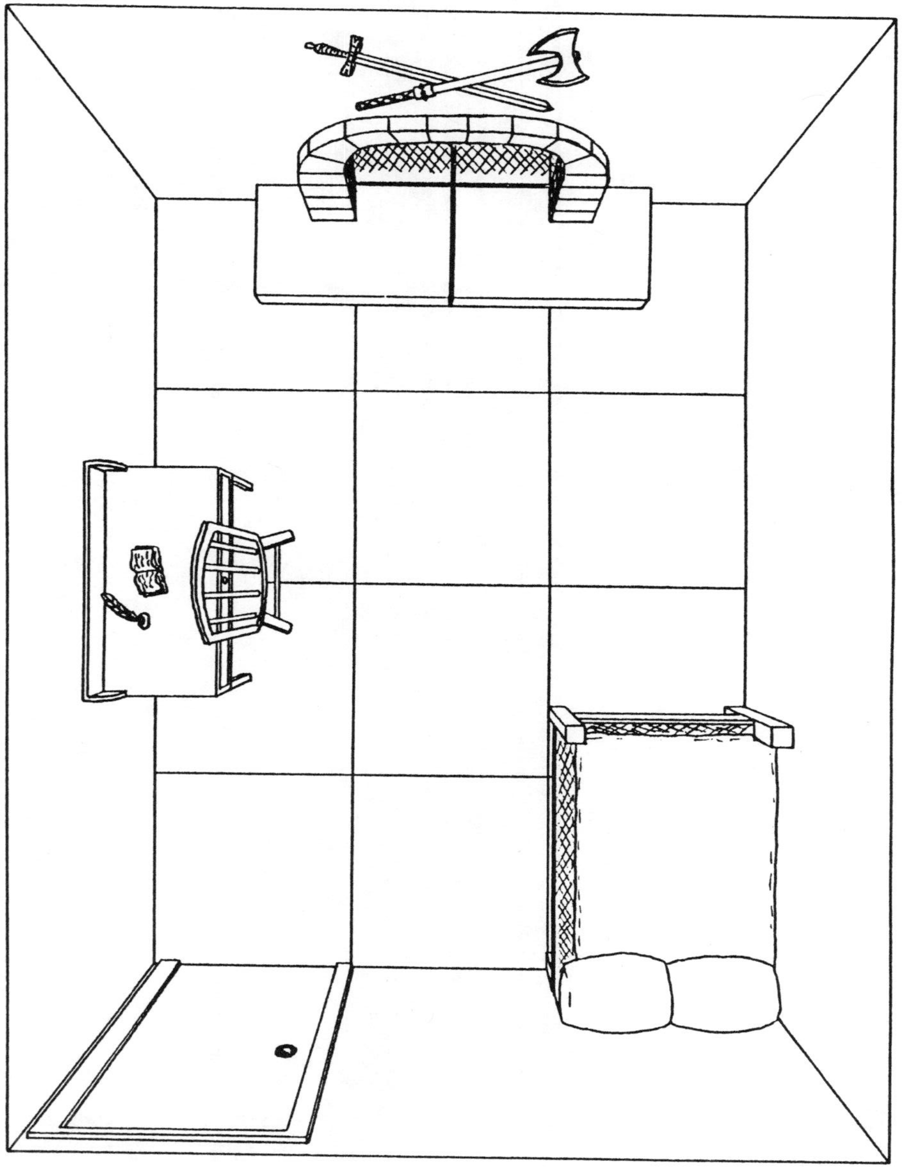

Relaxed I sit upon my perch
Till suddenly I give a lurch
And off I speed on wing-tips three
Before my prey can think to flee.
I make its flesh and tendons part
And claw my way into its heart.
Now only kin can set me free
So strike this cube with one of me.

Dilemma #2

The Impervious Cube

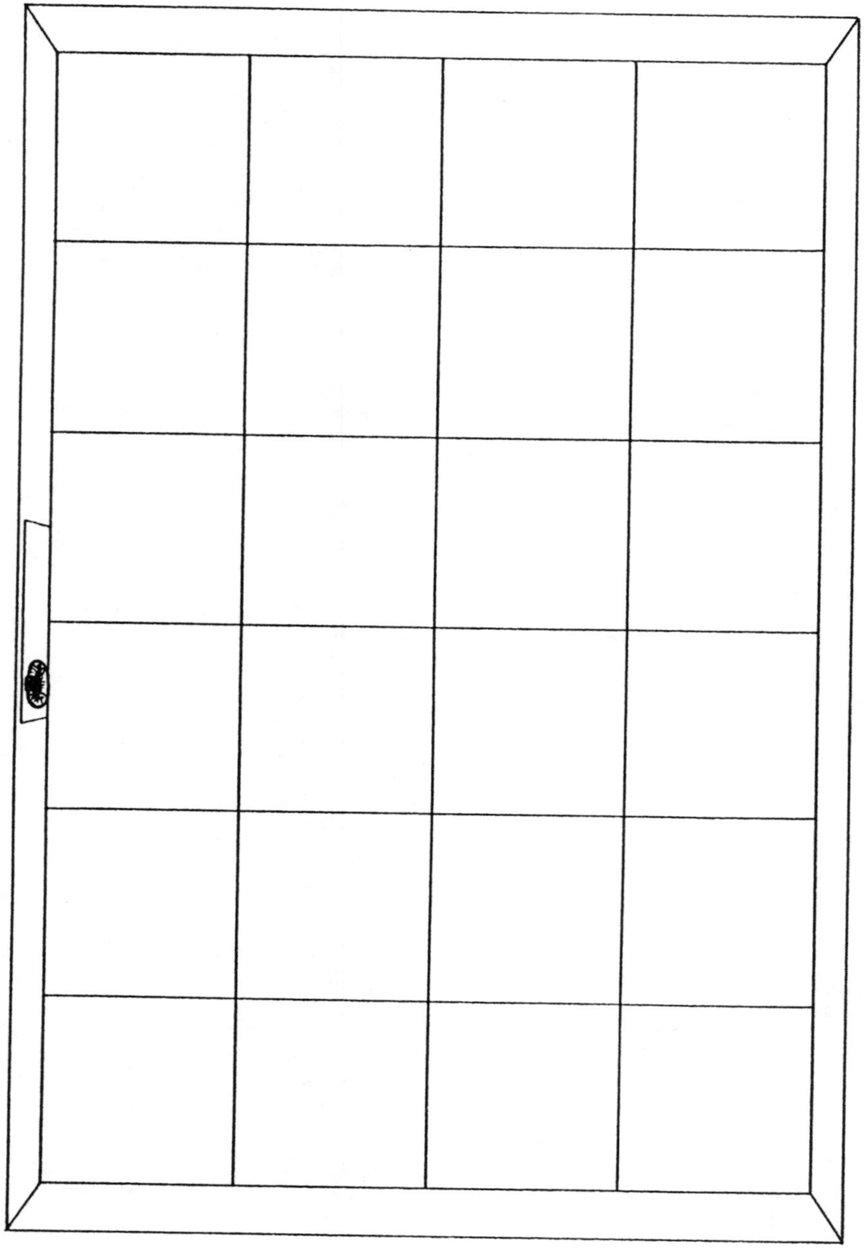

Dilemma #3

Lair of the Swarm

This 20' x 30' room is knee deep in bugs, obscuring any details of the floor and walls inside.

Carved into the stone door is a poem:

Rust Demise and Fire's Mirth,
Water Walker, Squeaking Dearth,
Wear me now upon your skin
And safely you may enter in.

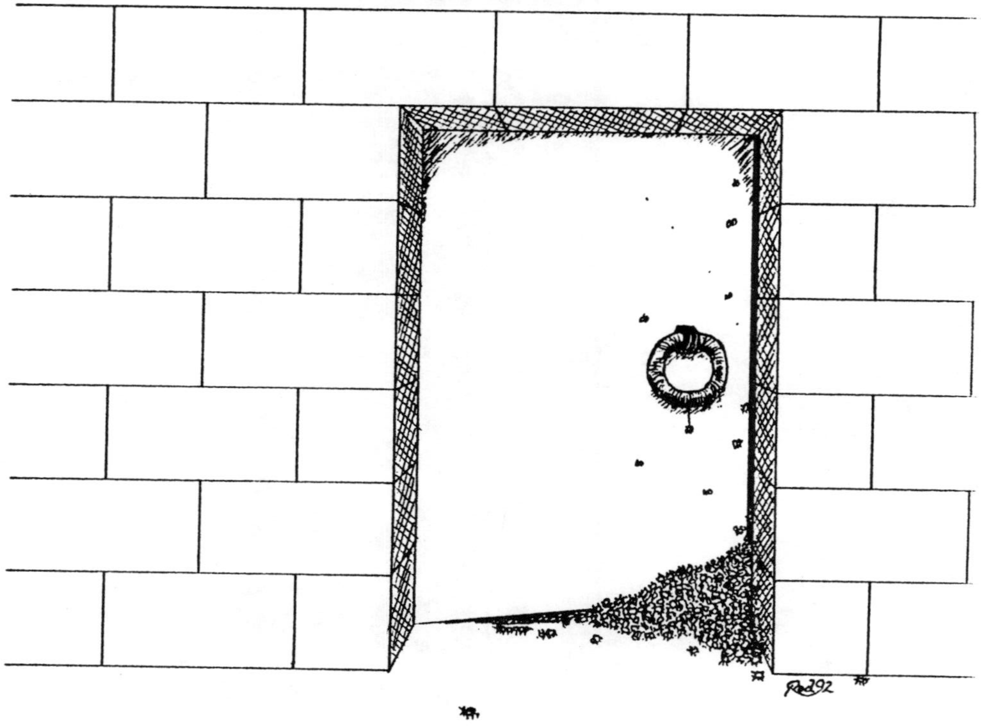

Dilemma #4 *The Greenhouse Effect*

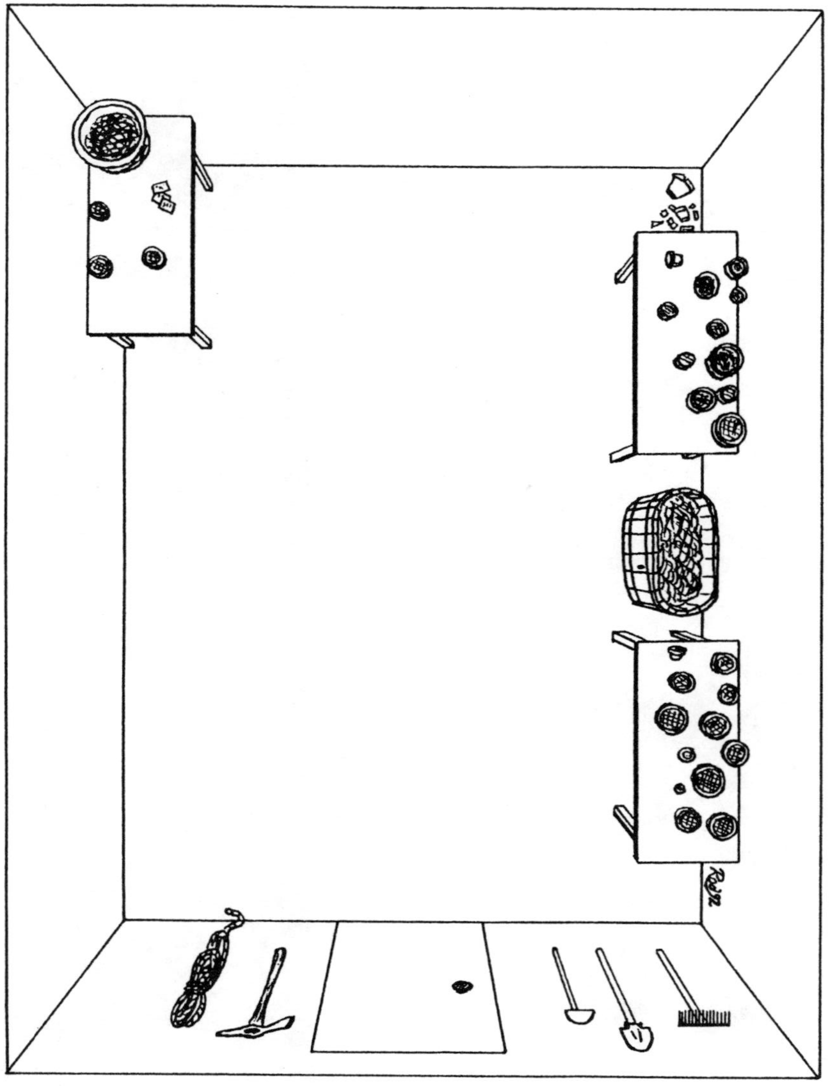

I ride the wind, I sail the sea,
I travel underground.
I nest in bird and fish and tree --
In everything I'm found.
Sometimes I sink into a hole
And wind up stranded there
But soon I overrun the bowl
Or take again to air.
I sneak into the smallest crack
To split a stone in twain.
Without a top or front or back
I never can be slain!
So place me all around the floor,
You won't believe your eyes.
Or turn around, go through the door,
And so forego your prize.

Dilemma #5
Wishing Well

Carved into the bucket are the words:

More valued than gold, more precious than silk,
Pouring like wine, flowing like milk.
A count's nightly feast, an offering of war,
A pact is now sealed, forever more.

Dilemma #6 *Hall of Flame*

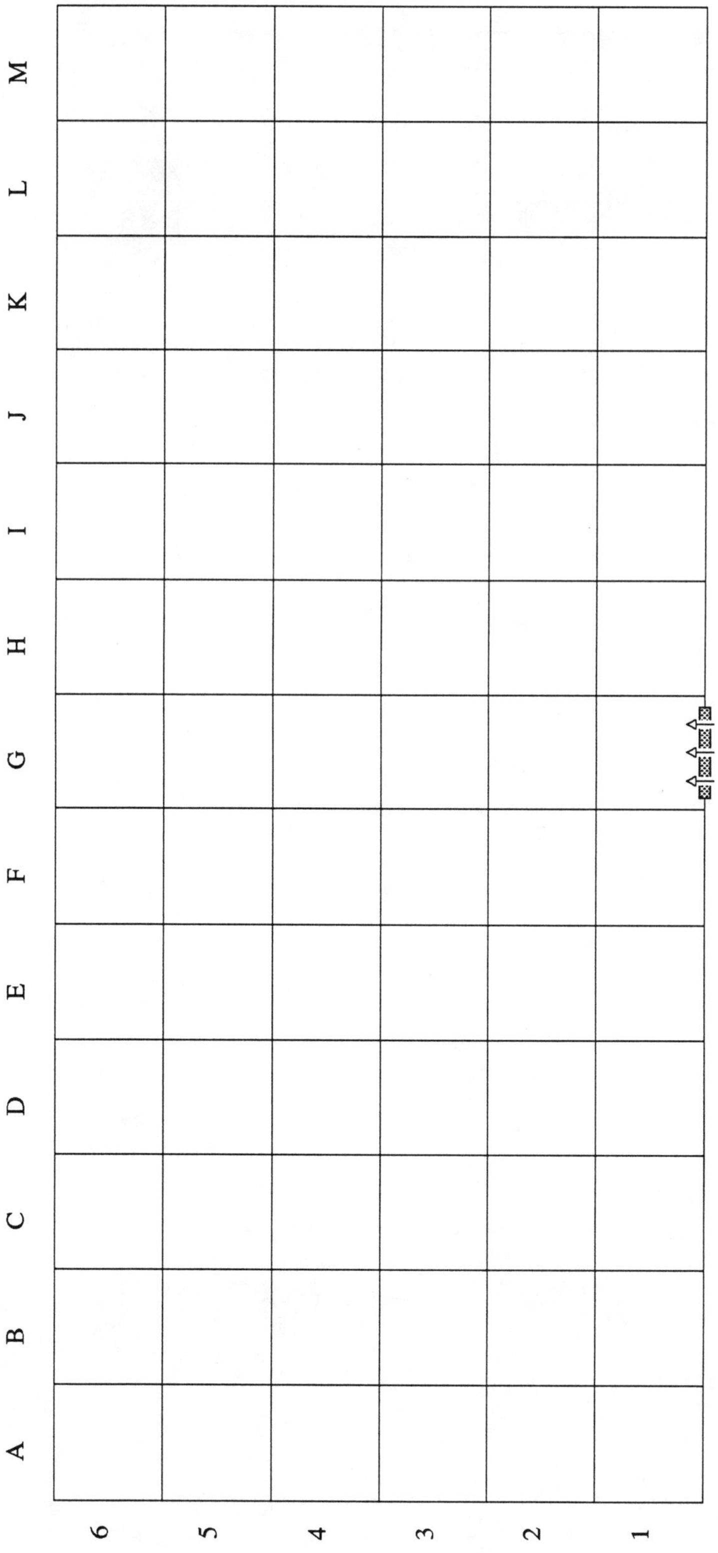

The door to this room (square G-1) is made of heavy stone and is hot to the touch. Chiseled into the door is:

> A nasty little maze have we
> To hurt you on your way
> Ignore the things that you can see
> And do just what I say
>
> Turn left and step, then one step more,
> Then pivot to the right,
> Step once, then twice, turn left, move four,
> Your goal is now in sight.
>
> Turn left again and step just twice,
> You're there without a doubt!
> Turn right and step and in a trice,
> You're safely headed out.

When you open the door, you see that the floor is made of red square paving stones. From all of the stones except the one directly in front of you, searing flames shoot up to the ceiling.

You can see no other exits through the inferno.

Dilemma #7
Grandma's Sitting Room

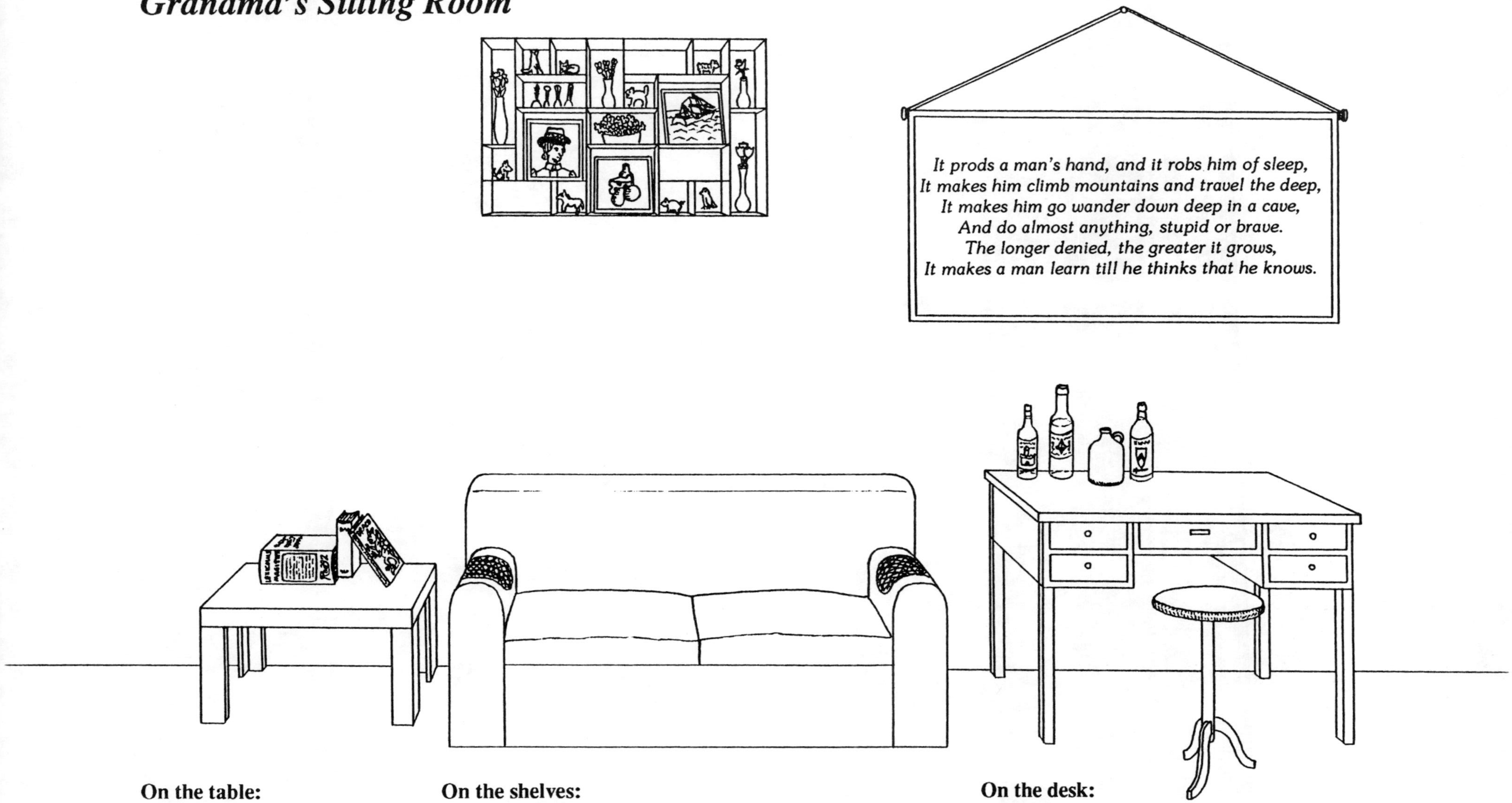

It prods a man's hand, and it robs him of sleep,
It makes him climb mountains and travel the deep,
It makes him go wander down deep in a cave,
And do almost anything, stupid or brave.
The longer denied, the greater it grows,
It makes a man learn till he thinks that he knows.

On the table:
Dictionary
Novel
Book of Dragons

On the shelves:
Flowers: rose, tulip, daffodils, marigolds, snapdragons
Ivory figures: cat, dog, fox, lamb, pig, pony, raven, wolf
Broken spoons: of silver, gold, brass and jade
Paintings: old woman, ocean scene, still life

On the desk:
Wine
Mead
Apple juice
Water

Illustration # 7-A

Give your players this scroll when they solve Dilemma #7.

Use my beasties carefully
And very happy you will be.
Call them by their rightful name
Or none of them will be quite tame.

Break the beasties one by one –
They'll each come back when each is done.
If the beasties go awry
Broken they might stay and die.

Felix Sheep and Winsome Dog
Minxy Fox and Lovely Hog
Raven Fast and Sleepy Horse
And Lastly Cunning Wolf Of Course.

Dilemma #8 *At the Buzzer*

AN EBON SPIRIT RISES HIGH
CHILD OF AIR AND FIRE
BORN IN DEATH YET BY WIND BORNE
IT FLIES BUT DOES NOT TIRE
IT TAKES YOUR LIFE WITHOUT A WOUND
OF THAT YOU CAN BE SURE
AND THOUGH IT CLAWS INTO YOUR EYES
IT TOO MAY ALSO CURE
Rod 92

Dilemma #9

Perfect Harmony

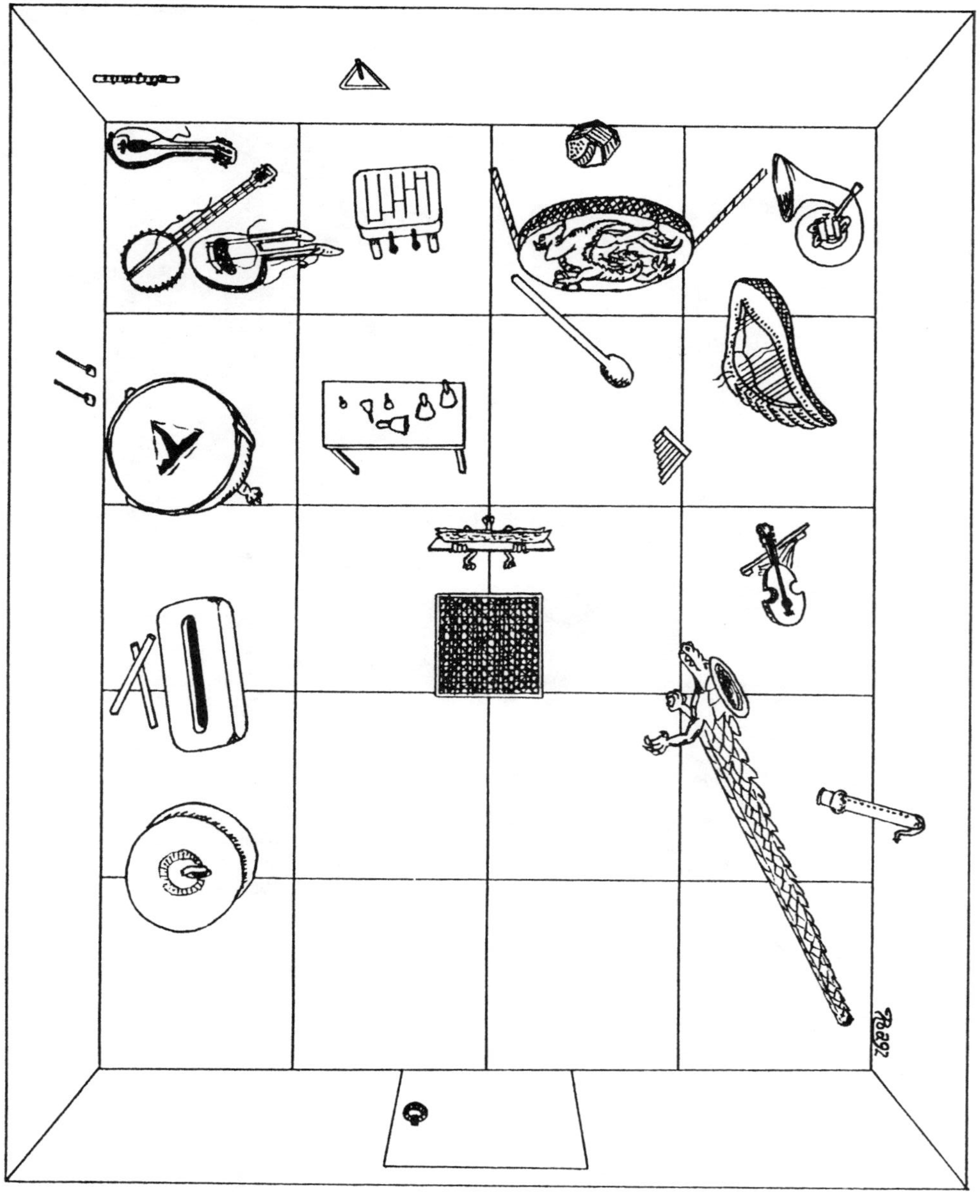

Back wall: flute, triangle on a rusty nail.

Back row: various broken stringed instruments, wooden percussion box, Gong hanging from ceiling by frayed rope, concertina with several keys missing and a dented zubaphone.

Second row: broken drum, various bells, pan pipes, harp with broken strings.

Third row: wooden drum, conductor's stand, smashed violin.

Fourth row: cymbals, dragon horn, oboe.

While separately each of us breaks
Together we can make a stand.
Entwined like countless tangled snakes
We form a strong, yet supple band.

Now call me by my rightful name
And tell me what to do.
Together we shall win great fame
And massive fortunes too!

Dilemma #10 -- Dead Men Tell No Tales

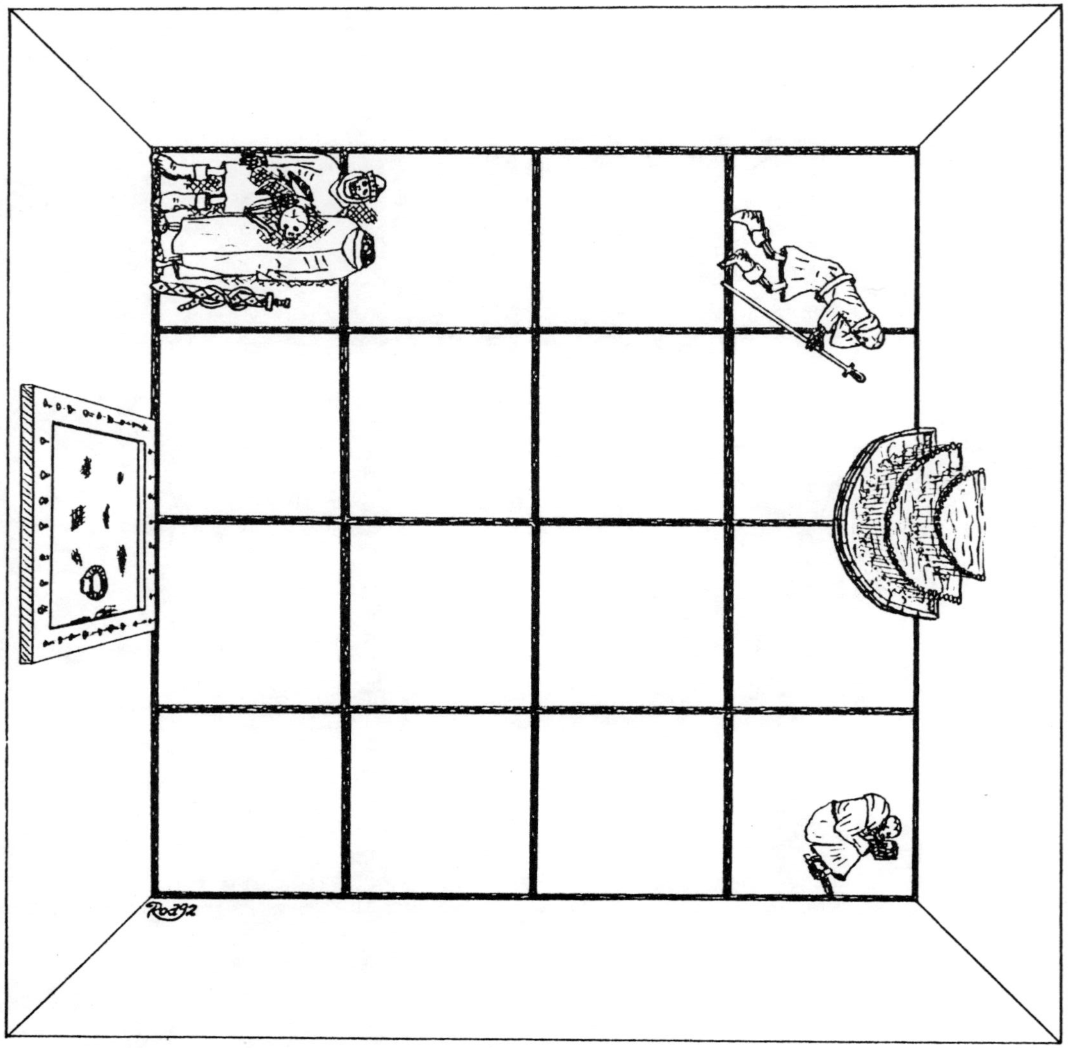

I lie here defeated, my life slips away,
Though I used to conquer this foe every day.
My killer's relentless and touches me now.
I know he'll succeed but to you I vow
Give me the weapon, after I've died,
I'll breathe once again and I'll tell what I spied.

Although the door to this room was blocked from the outside by a collapsed ceiling, you were easily able to enter. It's obvious that nobody inside could have forced their way out through the rubble.

The two skeletons to the left of the door died from obvious wounds. The cause of death for the other two is unclear. One of these -- evidently a monk -- holds a scrap of parchment on which a poem is written in blood.

Dilemma #11 — *Hidden Tomb*

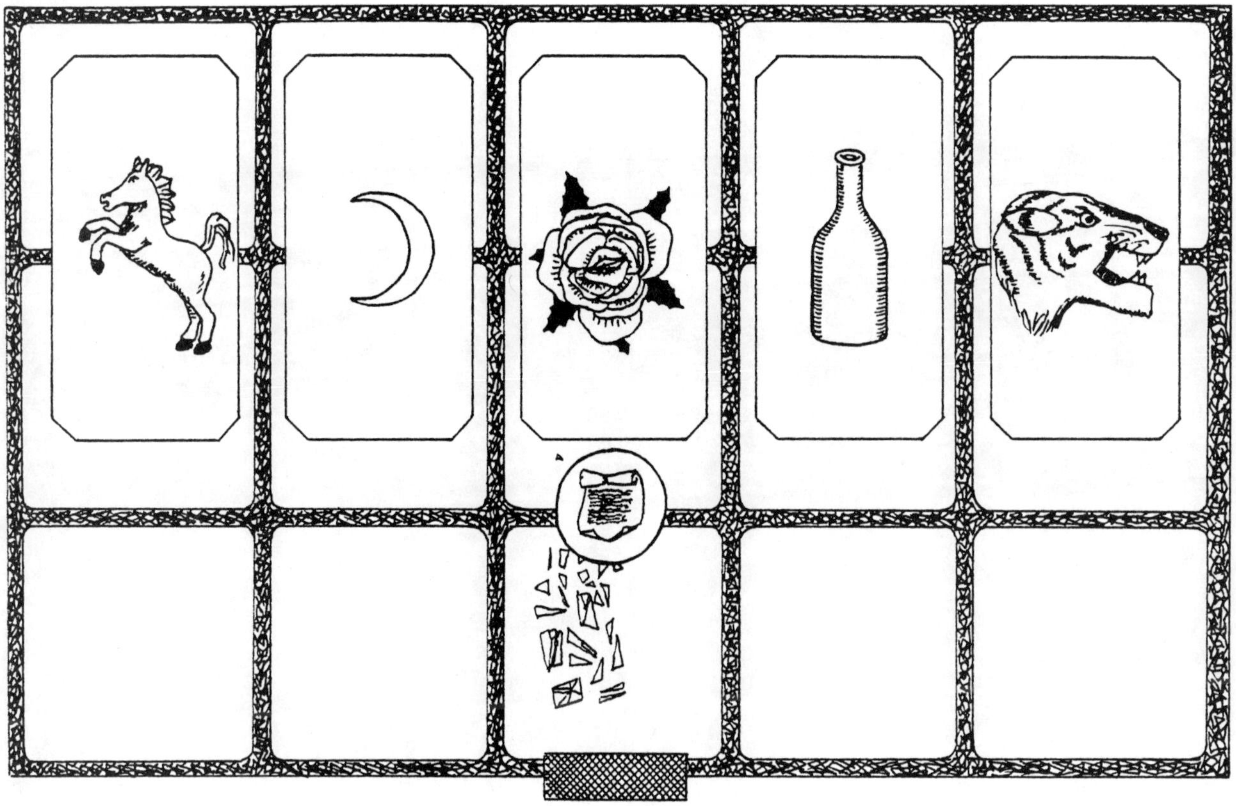

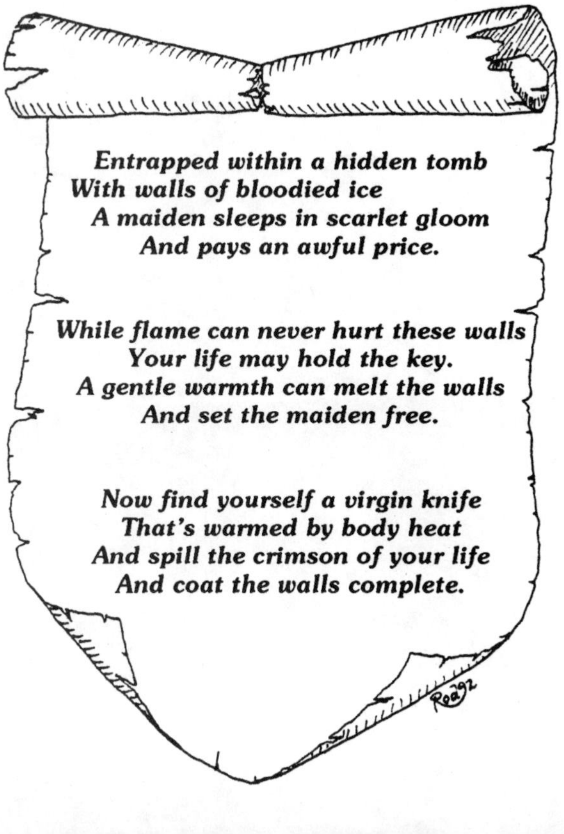
Entrapped within a hidden tomb
With walls of bloodied ice
A maiden sleeps in scarlet gloom
And pays an awful price.

While flame can never hurt these walls
Your life may hold the key.
A gentle warmth can melt the walls
And set the maiden free.

Now find yourself a virgin knife
That's warmed by body heat
And spill the crimson of your life
And coat the walls complete.

This 25' x 15' chamber contains five stone sarcophagi, a scroll and a broken mirror lying on the floor in front of the door.

Each of the sarcophagi has a heavy stone lid with a jewel inlaid:

Rearing Horse	Diamond
Crescent Moon	Ruby
Red Rose	Emerald
Red Wine	Sapphire
Tiger	Topaz

Dilemma #12
Knight Riders

On the outside of the door to this room are the words:

Move like a knight, you'll be all right
But use the greatest care
To plan it all and never fall
Upon a guarded square.

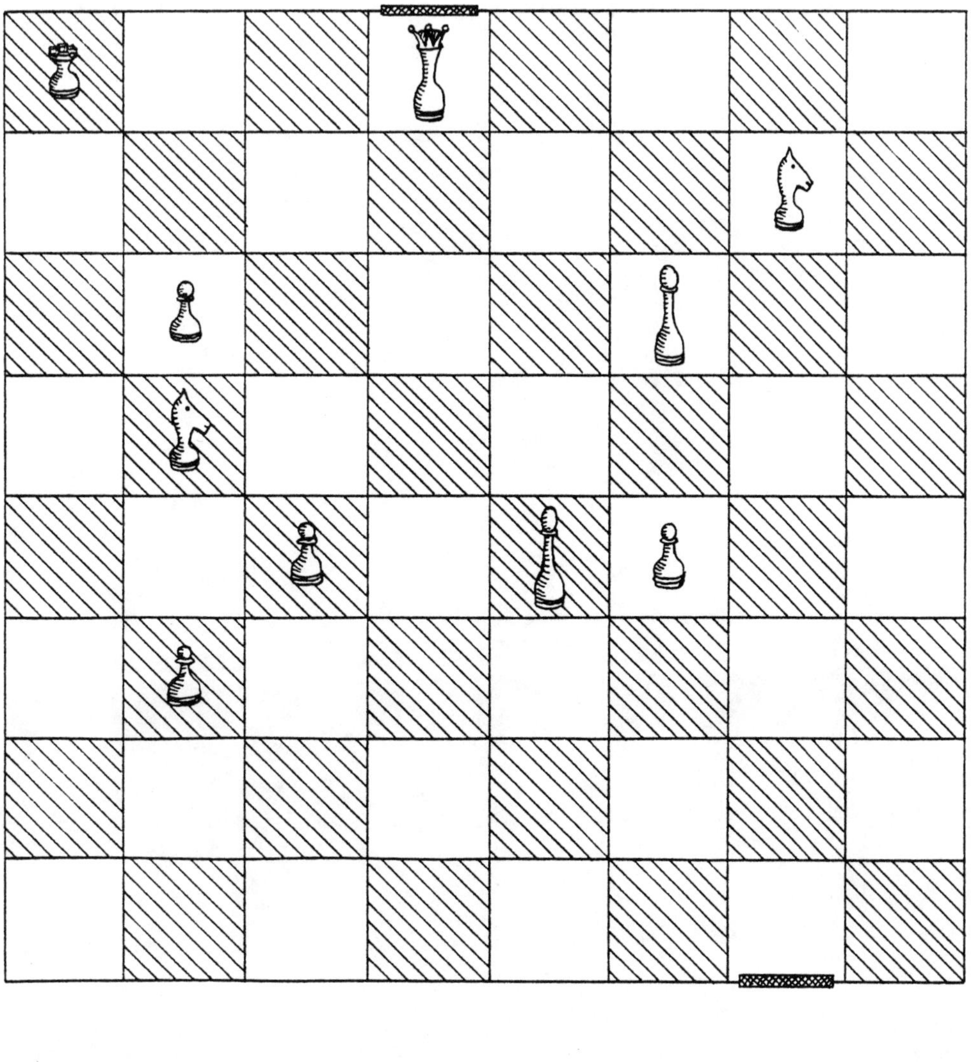

Dilemma #13 Warriors, Wyverns and Rocs

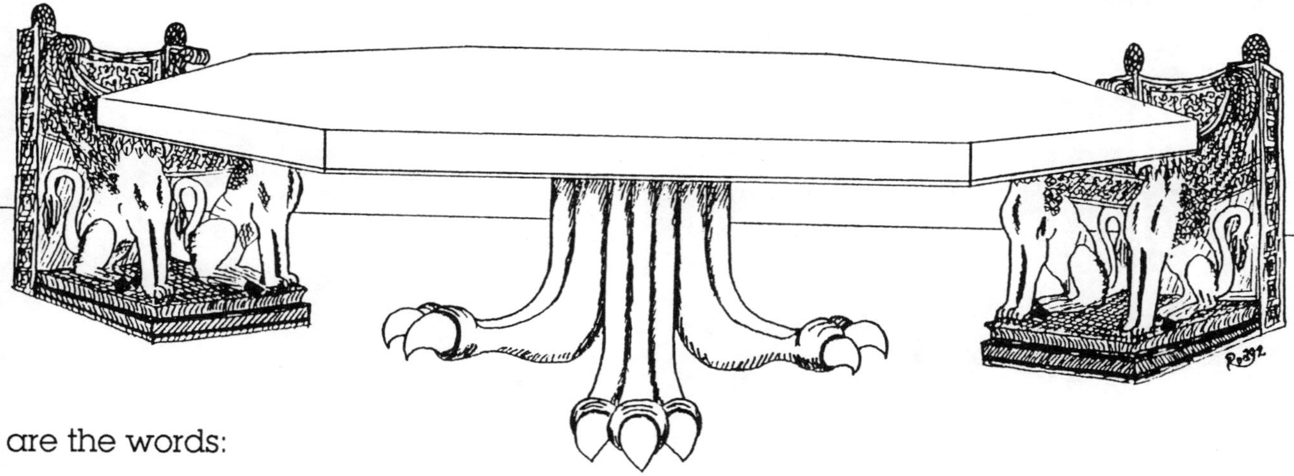

Graven in the table are the words:

I often have leaves, though I'm not a tree,
Sharp knives all around, I never do flee,
Though I'm often surrounded, I never feel fear,
A good turn in time, makes treasure appear!

Dilemma #14
Vanity

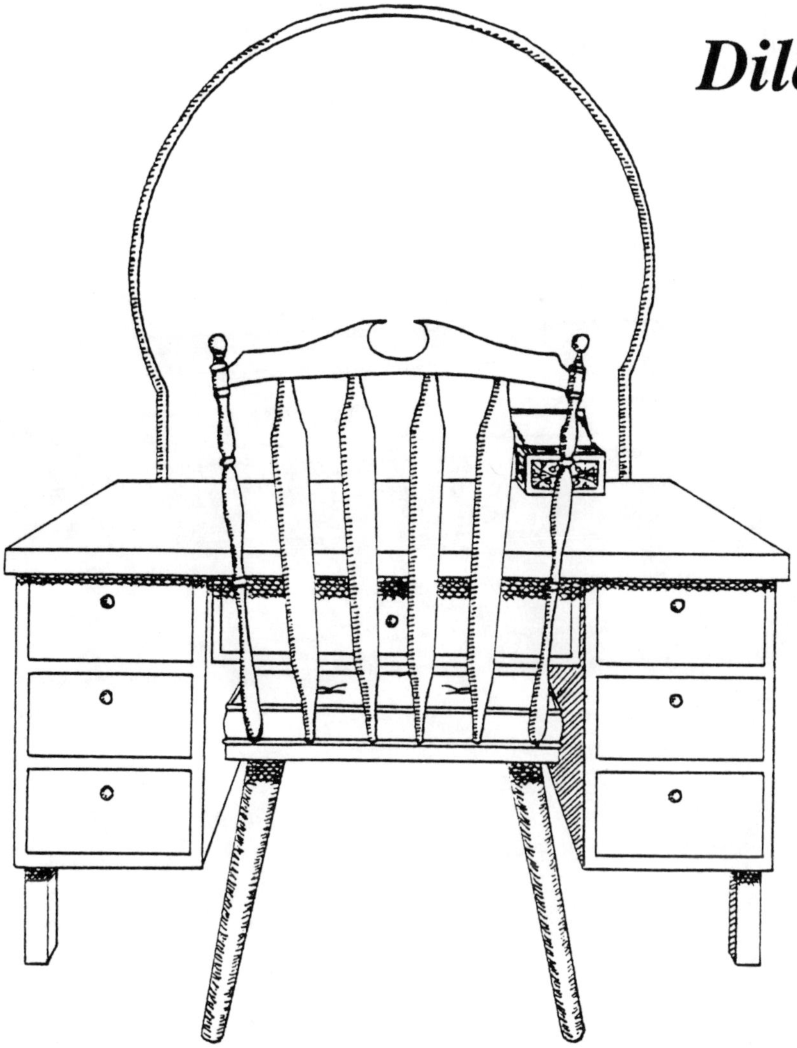

Etched in the top of the jewelry box is:

I turn to fog with mortal breath,
Or like a pond as still as death
I always tell to those who care
Who is ugly and who yet fair
There's one thing you should know, too,
When you look at me you look at you.

Dilemma #15

Doorways to Danger

Red key

Green key

Blue key

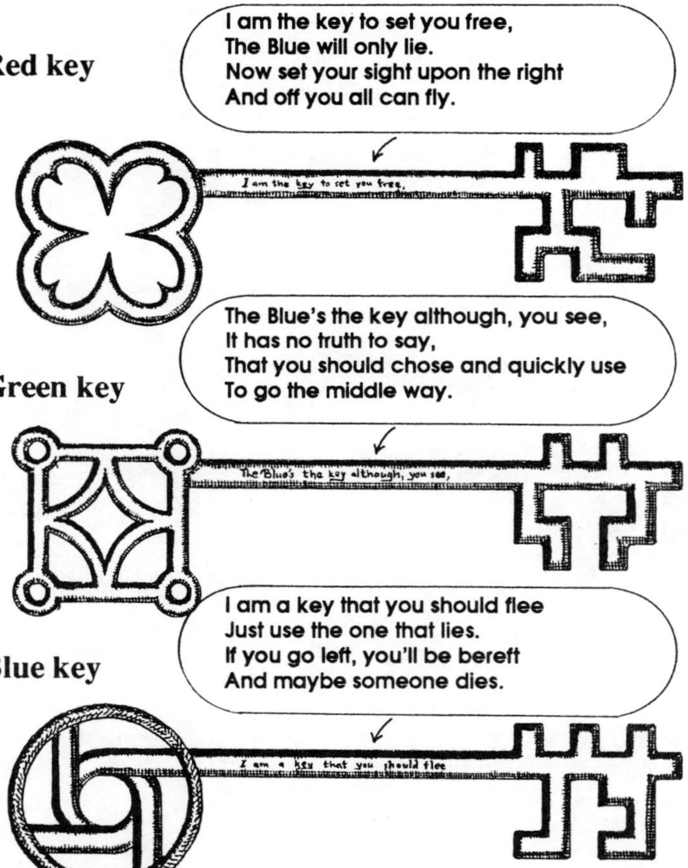
I am the key to set you free,
The Blue will only lie.
Now set your sight upon the right
And off you all can fly.
The Blue's the key although, you see,
It has no truth to say,
That you should chose and quickly use
To go the middle way.
I am a key that you should flee
Just use the one that lies.
If you go left, you'll be bereft
And maybe someone dies.

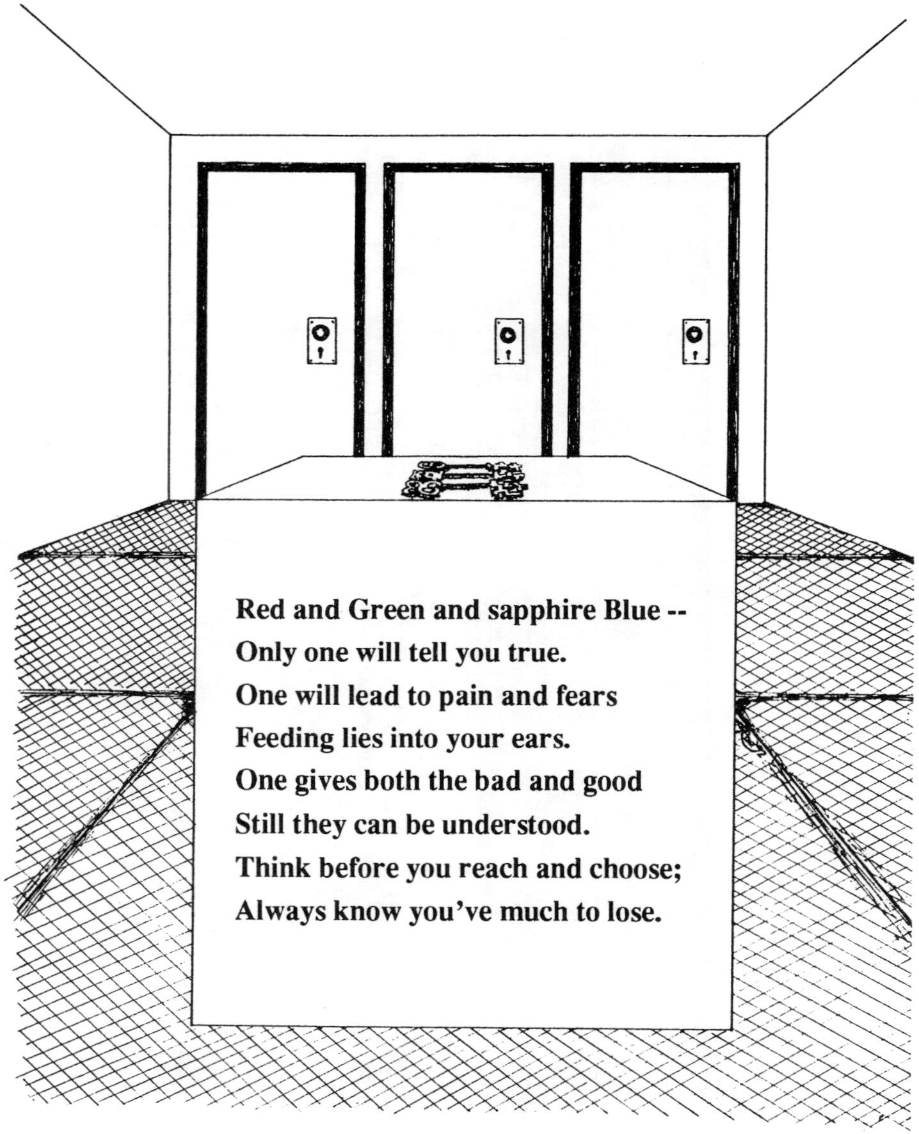
Red and Green and sapphire Blue --
Only one will tell you true.
One will lead to pain and fears
Feeding lies into your ears.
One gives both the bad and good
Still they can be understood.
Think before you reach and choose;
Always know you've much to lose.

Dilemma #16
Scared Senseless

The hexes in this room range from six feet below the entry hex to six feet above it. The ceiling is twenty feet above the entry hex. Written on the floor of the entry hex is a riddle:

The mirrors of your soul will say
That there is nothing here.
You tongue will also tell you nay
As will the sharpest ear.

Your fingers pass right through my skin --
There's nothing here to feel.
But find me now and stand within
And quickly you will heal.

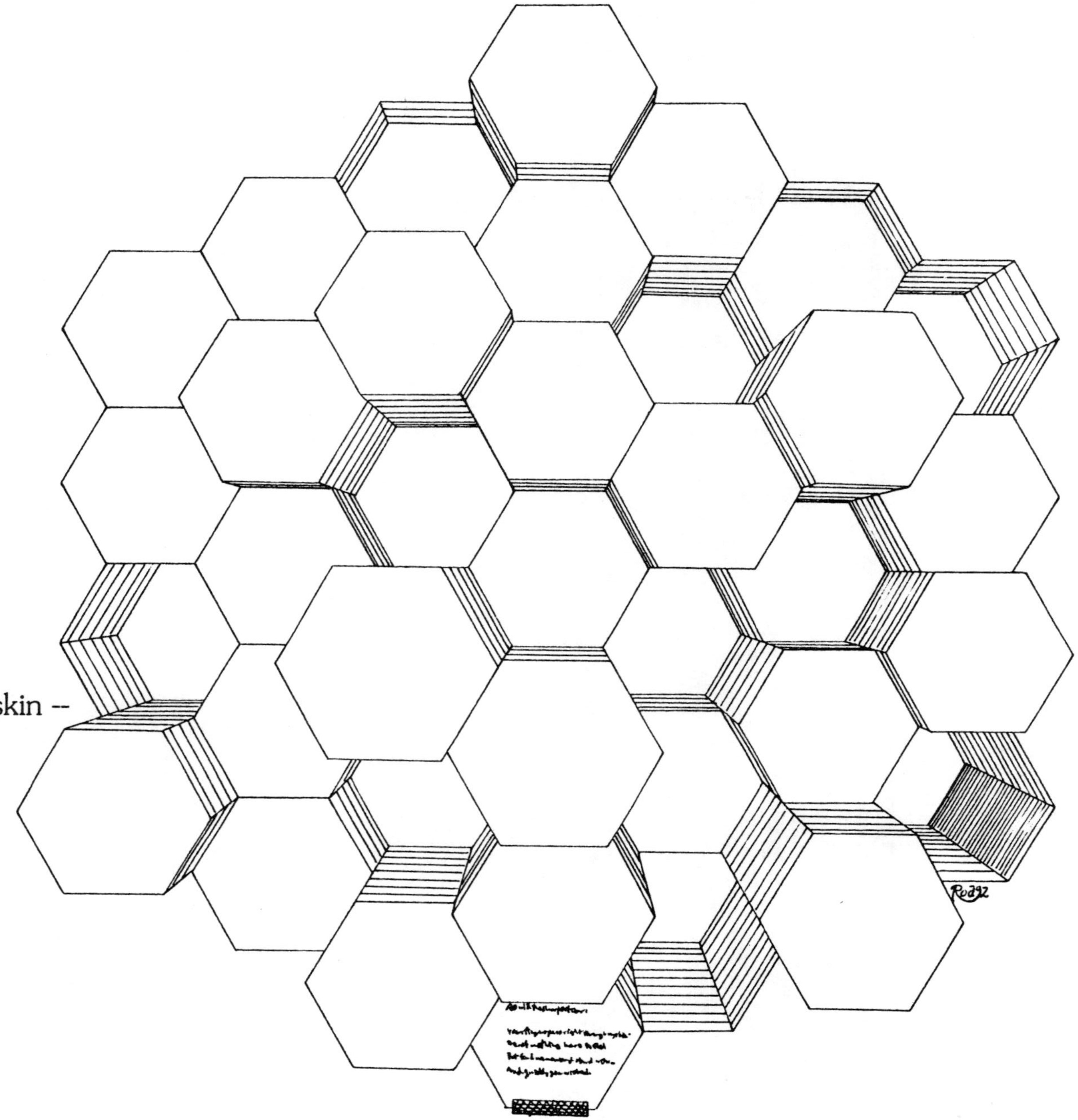

Dilemma #17
Wizard's Workshop

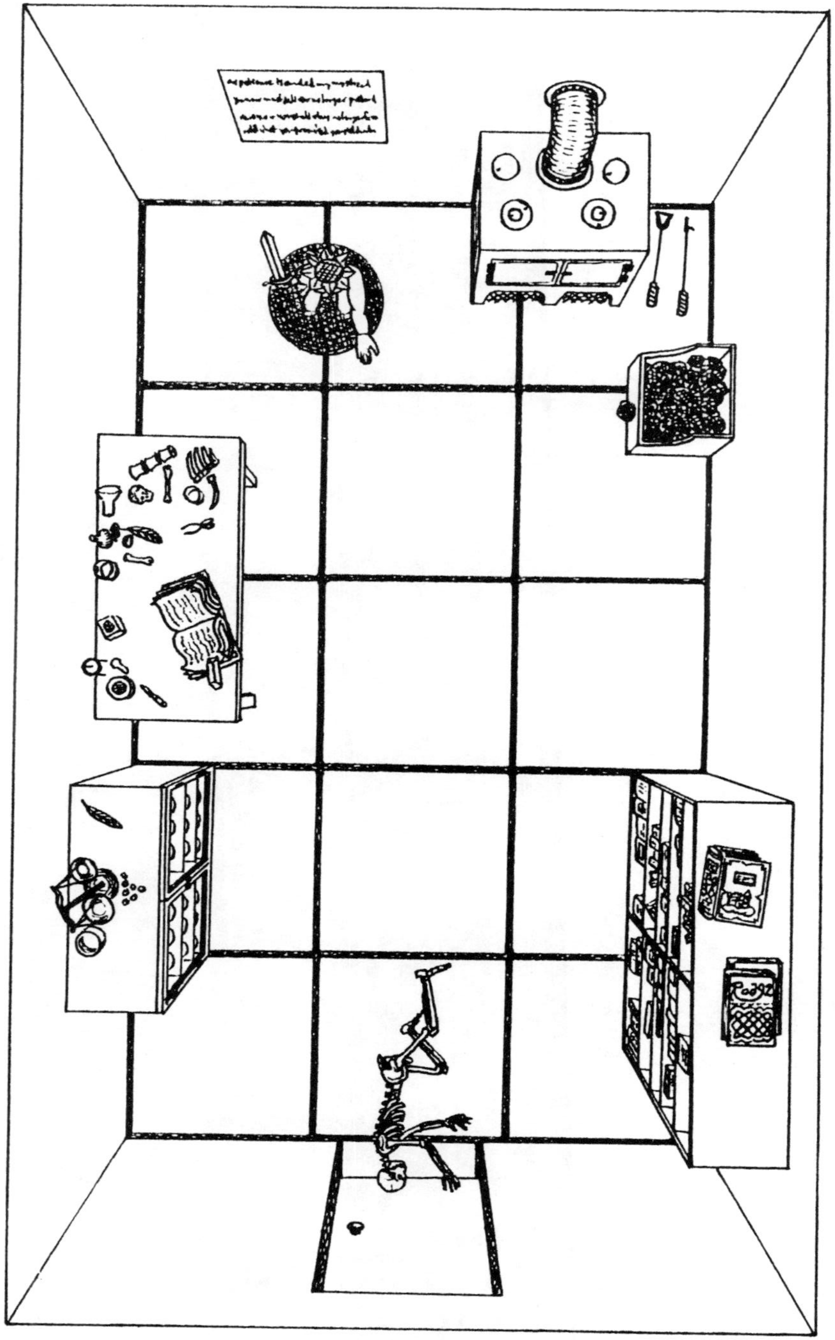

The door to this room was locked from the outside but was easily opened with a key hanging on the wall nearby. Inside the room is an alchemist's workshop. In front of the door is the skeleton of a human long dead.

Along the left hand wall is a cabinet containing several jars of liquid labeled honey, water and algae. There is a rusty old scale and a raven's feather on top of the cabinet. A workbench next to the shelves holds various gadgets, ribs and vertebrae from various creatures (including a dragon it seems), and a mangled book of magic with only one readable page.

Along the back wall is a statue of a king with an outstretched hand. In the corner is a furnace and a box full of coal. Near the right wall is a bookshelf filled with crumbling old books.

Written in the book on the workbench:

I am that which will never rust,
Between friends will erode trust,
Sunlight caught inside your hand,
Maker of Kings, destroyer of land,

From lead it comes, instead of mine,
By a secret hidden in the spine.

Written on the wall behind the statue:

My patience is ended, my mystical friend,
You now must deliver, no longer pretend,
Here you shall stay, no longer free,
Until what you promised, you yield unto me.

Illustration # 17-A

Give your players this scroll when they solve Dilemma #17.

Grind the dragon marrow well
Add some honey, make it gel.
Sift the coal and lead on top,
Mix five minutes without stop.
Magically bake for half an hour –
Shiny yellow starts to flower.

Dilemma #18   Pendants

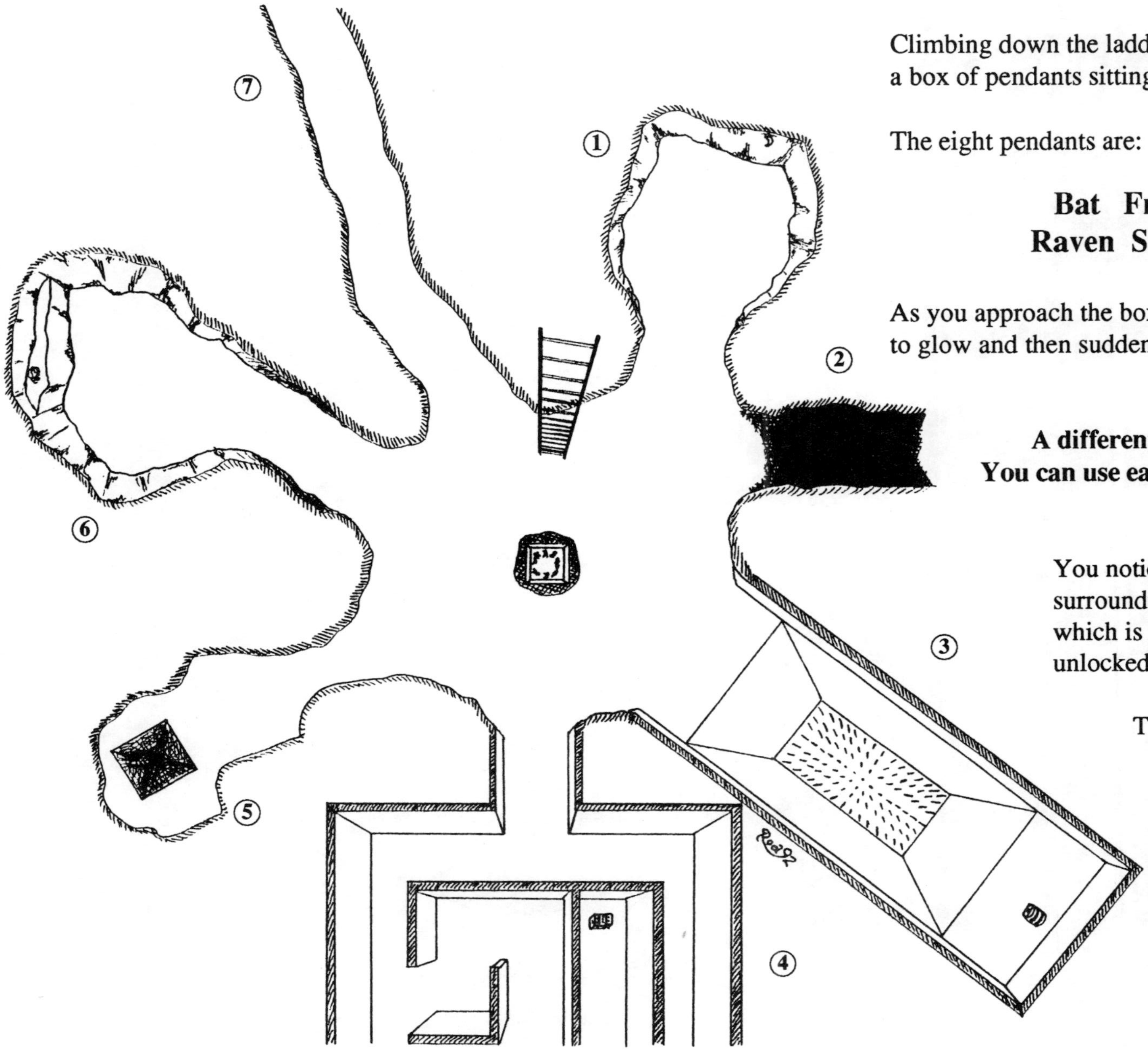

Climbing down the ladder into this chamber, you see a box of pendants sitting on a stalagmite.

The eight pendants are:

Bat Frog Giraffe Rat
Raven Spider Whale Wolf

As you approach the box, the Raven pendant begins to glow and then suddenly speaks:

A different helper, one per door
You can use each once, then Nevermore!

You notice there are seven alcoves surrounding the chamber, each of which is reached through a simple unlocked door.

The seven alcoves contain:

(1) A Crystal moon
(2) Very dark passageway
(3) 20' wide chasm
(4) A complex maze
(5) A deep, dark pit
(6) A sheer wall
(7) A long, airless passage

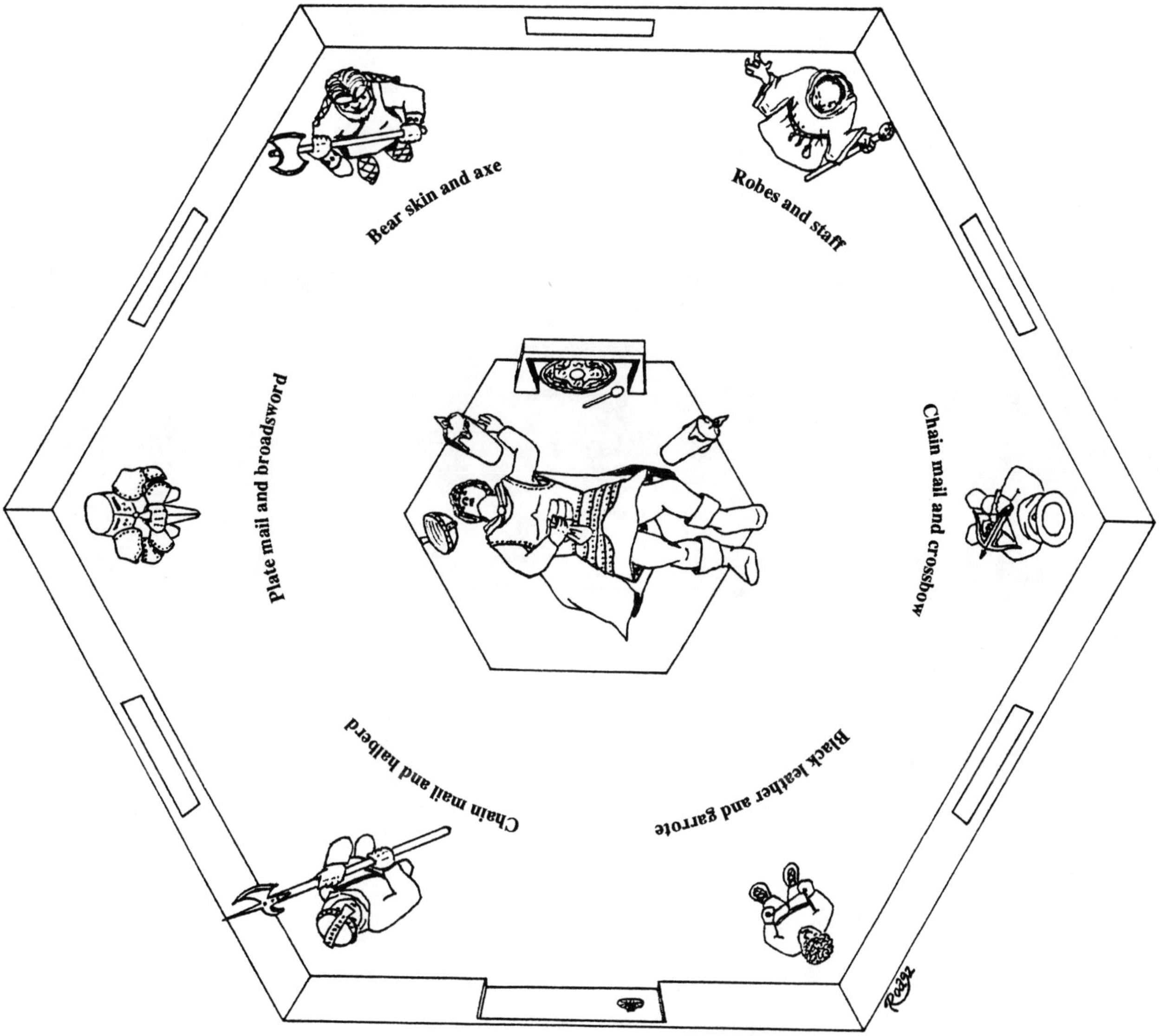

Dilemma #19
Crypt of Charon

Inscribed into the altar are the words:

Find the key 'ere the Darkness is filled.
Empty, yet waiting for when Life is stilled.
Enter and rest, with Charon's toll
Held fast and sure to the Windows of the Soul.
Sound the gong in the dead of the night.
Be wary, stray not, on your Stygian flight.
Take only that to which Earth belong
'Ere the Shadow o'er all begin his Dark Song.
Once only you may try to go free with one Goal.
Else hapless you'll roam in the Pit of Sheol.

On the altar are two tall candles, both lit, a corpse, a large gong and a hammer.
The corpse is fresh and seems to have wounds made by weapons like those held by the statues.

Dilemma #20
Shadowman!

Room contents, clockwise from the door:

A locked door through which you entered.
A small rug nailed to the floor.
A night table with an oil lamp on it.
A queen sized bed.
A marble statue of a snake charmer.
A glass case with a key inside.
A small fountain containing fish, small plants, shells, and pebbles.
A rusty suit of armor holding an extremely sharp battle axe.
A small wooden chair.
A cushioned chair.
A small chest.

Hanging over the center of the room is:

A glass chandelier suspended 40 feet above the floor by a chain bolted 13 feet from the floor.

The Perilous Potion

When red and orange fill the sky
And daylight's glow is fading,
I raise my bow and fiddle high
And start my serenading.

A single note is all I play,
The tempo's all I vary.
I'm somber on a chilly day
But when it's warm I'm merry.

A drop of blood from tongueless one
Is how this potion is begun
Two bloodless ones of gold and red
A verdant soldier burned and dead
A prize still in the armor plate
That's kissed by soldier standing straight
Now sweeten this for hours three
Til more you look and less you see
Put four legs in, then let him go
And add an ace and stir it slow
Add last a bit of golden hair
And drink the mixture if you dare.
A potion good to make you strong.
A potion fell if aught is wrong.

As still as death with baited breath
He waits with lidless eye.
As cold as stone he waits alone
For prey to happen by.

And in a blink too quick to think
He strikes with lightening speed
And by and by the prey will die
And then it's time to feed.

Legless runs beneath the trees
Tongueless murmurs to the breeze
Never sleeps within its bed
Cold as death but isn't dead.

First have no legs -- cannot swim,
Then grow one leg, fit and trim,
Soon enough I grow two more,
Next have five, then only four.

Our army marches 'cross the field
So thickly that we hide the dirt,
A million verdant blades we wield
Which cut but deal little hurt.

A straight standing soldier
From his crest to his toe,
Combating all darkness,
His primary foe.
Though 'tis unfair
It's the profession he chose,
The longer he fights
The shorter he grows.

Time doth it sweeten, as it sweetens time,
Love it enhances it's skill is sublime,
Loosens the tongue as it quickens the heart,
Thieves, Saints, and Kings to each it plays part.

In any weather we can thrive --
We flow across the plain,
And since we never are alive
We never can be slain.

Our presence you will never lack --
We never leave for long.
You chop us down -- we grow right back
An army thousands strong.

Beneath the drowsy summer sun
I spread my golden hair.
From dawn until the day is done
I lie without a care.

My locks soon turn from gold to white
And so departs my ease.
My hair comes loose and takes to flight
Adrift upon the breeze.

I guard my prize from squirrel fates
With sturdy armor all around
Until it's time to spread my plates
And drop my charges to the ground.

Upon my wings of rainbow lace
I soar upon the summer breeze
To hunt a noisome flying ace
Who stabs and drinks and spreads disease.

Just once a day I show my face
And once a day away I flee
And while I'm found without a chase
The more you look the less you see.

Within my veins no blood will flow
Yet I am quite alive.
I bask in Summer sunshine's glow
And for a while I thrive.

But when the chilly winds blow I,
Bedecked in gold and red,
Will tumble from my station high
And join the many dead.

A few have two, and many none,
A few have eight, but none have one,
The most have six, and lots have four,
A few have many, many more.

Housed in crumbling temple,
unseen by the eye,
Eternal and breathless, never to
die.
It's said that I'm lost if your life's
goal is greed,
Treasure's you've stored up that
I'll never need.

I'm never orange,
Though yellow can be.

A bard's good friend,
In his songs you find me.

In a child's book kept,
And in ballads too,

I'll bet you're surprised
Not to find me right here!

Born of the union of water and sun,
A marvel of beauty if ever was one.
A cloak of majesty worn by the sky,
No one can touch it but all dreamers try.

WITHOUT A MOUTH

YET I CAN TALK.

THE MOUNTAINS ARE MY HOME,

THROUGH THE HILLS I WALK,

THROUGH THE HILLS I,

THROUGH THE HILLS,

THROUGH THE,

THROUGH!

Other Cloud Kingdom Games Products

Riddle Rooms #2,
Wilderness Puzzles & Perils
Twenty more Riddle Rooms, in outdoor, wilderness and town settings. Some are deceptively simple; others are fiendishly complex. *96 pages. #50202*

Riddle Rooms #3,
Past, Present & Future
20 new illustrated encounters each posing a riddle or challenge. The rooms can be placed in fantasy, modern, or futuristic settings, and some in all three. *128 pages. #50203*

Lair of the Sphinx, A Riddle Book
77 Original and challenging riddles. Solve by yourself or with friends and family using the unique hint and explanation system. *144 pages. #50301*

Tower of the Riddle Master,
A Riddle Book
Challenge yourself to more of our original riddles. Can you solve them? Can you even find all 79? *144 pages. #50302*

Thieve's Island,
A Riddle Rooms Adventure
Thieves Island is a self-contained gaming scenario. Run our characters or yours through a series of puzzles, riddles and traps in an effort to get the treasure and get off the island - alive. *96 pages, 4-8 players. #50250*

Altered Images,
A Riddle Rooms Adventure
Your party must try to rescue the prince. But is that what you really want to do? Deceptions and intrigue abound as you race to save or slay the hostage. *96 pages, 4-6 players. #50251*

Castle of Magic
Castle of Magic is a fantasy role-playing board game. Each player has secret goals that the others can discover -- if they're clever enough. Work and win together if you can find players with compatible goals, or go for it all yourself. *4-6 players. #50010*

For additional information: www.CloudKingdom.com
e-mail: info@CloudKingdom.com